DINING AT DUSK

Evening eats-
Tapas, Antipasti, Mezze, Ceviche
and Aperitifs *from* Around *the* World

STEVAN PAUL

with photographs by
Daniela Haug

whitecap

DINING AT DUSK

PREFACE: Stevan Paul   PHOTOS: Daniela Haug

In an ideal world, I'd envisage a sunny day in mid-May
for this journey on the heels of the sun as it sets around the globe.

PREFACE

The approaching dusk starts with a unique light, when a golden
evening glow gradually blends into slowly darkening blue skies.
A mild breeze might make its way through streets, alleys and
gardens, gently cooling roofs and terraces still hot from the day's sun.

Lights start coming on everywhere. The evening begins to take on colour as the city's noise softens, merging with the first beats of the night's music. There's laughter, clinking glasses, *joie de vivre*. Saucepans are moved onto cookers, fires are lit. Aromas of herbs and spices waft through the streets – not long now before there will be a bite to eat!

Dining at dusk is magical. The day's work is done. We can let go and make time for a cool drink, accompanied by small, uncomplicated dishes. It's time to clock off. Time for friends and family. Time to gather and enjoy. It's the perfect time for stories, for listening, talking, marvelling and laughing.

I have experienced this magic time and again during my culinary travels: all over the world, people gather around the blue hour, meet at bars, food counters, pubs, izakayas, bodegas and bistros, at cervejarias and tapas bars for a drink, a few snacks and nibbles. It's relaxed and full of joy.

Many countries around the world have a distinctive bar food culture that forms an essential part of their culinary heritage. From Italian cicchetti, Spanish tapas and Greek mezze through to British pub food and well beyond, to Portugal, Latin America and Mexico, with tacos, tortillas and ceviche, across the Caribbean to India, China and Australia – everybody loves quickly and easily prepared delicacies shared with friends and guests in a casual environment, whether at home or at a bar or party. Moreover, these snacks are surprisingly light and healthy, with plenty of fresh herbs, salads and vegetables, some of them vegetarian or even vegan, some with high-quality fish and grilled meats. We find exciting combinations with intriguing spices, new aromas and the typical flavours of national cuisines.

In this book, we follow the course of the setting sun on a culinary journey around the world for the golden hour, introducing us to delightful snacks, nibbles, delicacies, bar and finger foods. Uncomplicated treats are served with a generous side of music, an essential part of any sunset. This book therefore invites you a musical journey as well as a culinary one, with suggestions ranging from sophisticated jazz and lounge music to soul and funk, Latin and Brazilian tunes, chansons and beautiful traditionals.

The old often meets the new as the dusk approaches, and contemporary cuisine for this beautiful time of the day is a true discovery: relaxed, simple and comforting at any time of the day and a perfect match for modern life.

I hope you'll enjoy this exciting culinary journey through dusk-time dining all over the world. The evening belongs to us – as does the day!

STEVAN PAUL

THE
NIGHT
IS STILL
YOUNG

OKA I'A

Fish salad

INGREDIENTS

(serves 4)

300–400 g fresh cod, deboned

½–1 red chilli

Juice of 1 lime

Salt

1 organic Lebanese cucumber

150 g grape tomatoes

1–2 spring onions

1 small red onion

20 g fresh ginger

150 ml (⅔ cup) unsweetened coconut milk

4–6 sprigs coriander (cilantro)

Optional: edible flowers (in the photo: thyme and chives flowers)

Days on Samoa, the tiny island state in the south-western Pacific, begin on the east coast of Upolu Island, on the heavenly beaches of Lalomanu. There, sunrises are just as spectacular as the sunsets, when the skies above the Polynesian islands start to glow in rich blue, golden orange and fiery red hues. It's the perfect time for a bowl of oka i'a, a traditional Samoan fish salad that combines the delicate acidity of South American ceviche (p. 207) with the mild creaminess of Hawaiian poke.

———

Dice the fish flesh into bite-sized pieces. Mince the chilli, removing the seeds if you prefer less heat. Combine the minced chilli, lime juice and diced fish. Season with salt, cover and set aside to marinate for at least 30 minutes.

Slice the cucumber, season with salt and set aside. Slice the grape tomatoes thickly and sprinkle with a little salt. Cut the spring onions into fine rings. Set aside a little of the green rings for garnish. Peel the onion, finely dice and season lightly with salt. Grate the ginger and stir into the coconut milk together with a pinch of salt.

Remove the fish from the lime marinade and drain. Transfer to a bowl together with the remaining ingredients and top with the coconut milk. Divide among plates. Garnish with the reserved spring onions, picked-off coriander leaves and the flowers, if using, and serve.

— MANUIA! —

Samoans like to drink kava, a non-alcoholic, yet calming to mildly intoxicating beverage made of yaqona, the dried, powdered roots of the pepper plant, combined with water and traditionally served in wooden bowls. However, this dish also goes well with a New Zealand Sauvignon Blanc.

AUSTRALIA

Australia is a gourmet's paradise. The country stretches across six climate zones, making for an enormous variety of local produce. There is essentially no vegetable or fruit that is not grown on this vast continent – all in mouth-watering quality.

Local markets are the stuff of foodies' dreams, and Australian cuisine is shaped by indigenous ingredients, British culture and the culinary traditions of migrants from Europe, Asia, the Orient and Africa. These influences, plus the availability of superior regional produce from both land and sea, have fostered a highly creative, regionally oriented global cross-over cuisine that is as unpretentious, diverse and relaxed as Australians themselves.

People love eating from bar counters and food trucks, and around sunset they often gather to share delicious food over a craft beer or a chilled red from Margaret River, casually handed over the counter. We travelled through south-western Australia and stopped at No Mafia in Perth for sundown, where we were served char-grilled octopus (seasoned with salt and nothing else) on a subtly spicy chilli paste, drizzled with rosemary oil on a simple paper napkin. Just a few streets away, at the Darlings Supper Club, I relished a spicy char kway teow: fried noodles with Chinese sausage, prawns, chicken and juicy clams. I also loved the beef carpaccio with Pedro Ximénez sherry and harissa, served with

a mushroom doughnut and chives curd at The Standard. I met Eric Wong from the Noodle Forum, a middle-aged gentleman who straddles a bamboo pole to knead the dough for the best soup noodles I've ever tasted. We ordered jook-sing noodles with delicately seasoned BBQ pork, braised beef and bok choy, and green jook-sing noodles with spinach and roasted tofu.

Other memorable meals were the sandwiches at Toastface Grillah (p. 16), Jim Mendolia's freshly fished sardines at Fremantle Port (p. 25) and the wild salad we picked on the beach with Josh "Koomal" Whiteland, an Aboriginal man who would guide us to Ngilgi Cave later at night, a cathedral of stone as old as the world.

We visited vineyards and chatted with craft beer brewers. Everywhere we went, we encountered a spirit of community, of no one being worthier than the next guy. Farmers, producers, gastronomists – they all work together and recommend and praise each other. Maybe this is because competitive thinking is not so fitting for a country where virtually everybody has a migrant background.

UNPRETENTIOUS, EXCITING, RELAXED: AUSTRALIA

SUNSET WITH A VIEW

Australia has plenty of beautiful and even spectacular sunsets to offer. However, the colours are at their most intense at Uluru/Kata Tjuta National Park where the world-famous Uluru (Ayers Rock) glows fiery red in the evening sun underneath a deep blue sky dotted with pink clouds.

B.A.G.

Bacon, apple & Gouda sandwich

The sangas handed across the narrow counter of Toastface Grillah, a bar pounded by heavy basses and rap (the Grillah boys love hip-hop), are very possibly Perth's best grilled sandwiches. The bar's namesake, hip-hop legend Ghostface Killah (Wu-Tang Clan) stopped over in Perth on a tour in December 2014. When he was told about this little bar, he dropped by, the boys served him a few sandwiches, and the next day Ghostface gave a secret gig in the bar's back yard. The event was communicated via Facebook, and thousands came.

The sandwiches on the menu feature fun names with puns good enough to delight any hip-hop fan. We tried and enjoyed "Steak's High", a finger-licking good combination of pulled pork, chilli, cheddar and Italian Provolone cheese – a spicy, soft and creamy filling between freshly toasted slices of bread. Another great concoction is the "Notorious B.A.G." with smoky bacon, fresh slices of apple, melted Gouda and braised onions between crusty slices of toast. I sto… sampled the recipe straight away for this book.

HERE'S HOW (makes 2 sandwiches)

Slice **1 onion**. Heat **1 tbsp olive oil** over medium heat, add the onion, season with salt, and braise until golden brown, about 10–12 minutes. Once cooked, season the onions with **1 pinch piment d'Espelette** (mild red chilli powder). Preheat the oven to 200°C (390°F). Heat another large, non-stick pan (with a lid). Add **4 slices bacon** and fry slowly until crisp, turning occasionally. Peel ½ **small apple** and slice finely using a mandolin. Drain the bacon on kitchen paper. Add **20 g (1½ tbsp) butter** to the bacon fat in the pan and reduce the heat. Place **2 slices of bread** into the pan. Divide **80 g (¾ cup) grated Gouda cheese** on top of the bread slices and top with the bacon, sliced apple and braised onions. Season with freshly ground black pepper. Fry for 2–3 minutes until the bread has browned on the bottom. Top the sandwiches with **2 more slices of bread** and press together. Turn the sandwiches and continue to fry for another 2–3 minutes until golden brown on the other side. Transfer to the preheated oven on a tray lined with baking paper for another 5 minutes.

BOTTOMS UP!

A lovely Australian craft beer, perhaps from the Feral Brewing Company, 40 minutes drive from Perth. These sangas also go well with coffee!

CHICKEN NOODLE
BOWL

BUDDHA BOWL

BUDDHA BOWL & CHICKEN NOODLE BOWL

Buddha bowls or health bowls are very popular in Australia.
These healthy, filling meals in a bowl are renowned for their creative and
unconventional combinations of flavours and aromas from all over the world.
They are perfect embodiments of Australia's relaxed, international cuisine.

BUDDHA BOWL (makes 2–4 bowls)

Peel **1 organic Lebanese cucumber** into strips and
slice. Add **freshly minced red chilli** to taste. Finely
slice **1 red radish** using a vegetable peeler. Season
with salt.

Boil **150 g (⅔ cup) black lentils** in unsalted water
for 20 minutes. Drain, refresh under cold water,
add **1 tbsp olive oil** and season with salt.

Bring **100 g (½ cup) quinoa** to a boil in **300 ml
(1¼ cup) water**, add salt, cover and simmer for
10 minutes. Season with salt and **1 tsp nut oil** of
choice. Cover and set aside to absorb all the water.
Once cooled, add **150 g (1 cup) chickpeas** from
a tin, mix with the quinoa, and season with salt.

Peel **1 red onion** and cut into thin wedges.
Toss with **150 g (¾ cup) tinned corn** and **1 tbsp
olive oil**. Season. Cut **200 g smoked tofu** into
8 slices. Dry-roast **2 tbsp sesame seeds in a pan**.
Add **2 tbsp olive oil** and fry the tofu 2–3 minutes
on each side. Add **1 tbsp honey**, leave to bubble
up briefly and season.

For the vinaigrette, whisk the **juice of ½ lemon** with
4 tbsp rice vinegar, **2 tbsp mirin** (alternatively
honey), **6 tbsp olive oil** and **5 tbsp sweet soy sauce**.
Put the bowl together as shown in the photo. Drizzle
with the vinaigrette and garnish with fresh coriander
(cilantro) leaves.

CHICKEN NOODLE BOWL (makes 2–4 bowls)

Cut **1 tbsp dried wakame seaweed** very finely
with scissors. Transfer to a bowl, add hot water
and leave to swell. Drain, refresh under cold water
and drain again.

Boil **100 g (½ cup) yellow split lentils** in unsalted
water for 6 minutes, drain and refresh under cold
water. Pull **½ grilled chicken** (ready-made) into bite-
sized pieces. Boil **150 g soba noodles** in salted water
according to the instructions on the packet (mine
took 7 minutes). Drain and refresh immediately under
cold water. Drain again, season lightly and toss with
2–3 drops sesame oil.

For the vinaigrette, whisk **4 tbsp soy sauce** with the
juice of ½ lime, **1 tbsp mirin** (alternatively honey)
and **2 tbsp rice vinegar**. Add freshly minced **red
chilli** to taste. Finely chop **4–6 sprigs coriander** and
stir in. Dry-roast **2 tbsp sesame seeds** in a pan. Add
to the vinaigrette while still hot. Whisk the vinaigrette
with all ingredients and season to taste with salt.

MUSIC: *Melbourne band Hiatus Kaiyote serve a relaxed
musical feel-good bowl of neo-soul, jazz, hip-hop and
electronica with light-as-air basses and the smooth, yet
powerful voice of their lead singer and guitarist Nai Palm.*

REUBEN BREAD STACK WITH RED COLESLAW

INGREDIENTS

(makes 2 bread stacks)

For the red coleslaw:
400 g red cabbage
Salt
3–4 tbsp balsamic vinegar
1–2 tbsp marmalade
1 tbsp olive oil
1–2 drops toasted sesame oil
Freshly ground black pepper
8–12 pecan nuts

For the sandwiches:
1 red onion
Salt
Red wine vinegar
4 lettuce leaves
2 tbsp oil
4 slices fresh pineapple,
    not too thick
Chilli flakes
2 sprigs coriander (cilantro)
6 slices rye bread
2–3 tbsp wholegrain mustard
4 slices semi-mature Gouda
    cheese
8 slices pastrami
1 small jar gherkins

This version of a Reuben sandwich is typical of Australian chefs' relaxed, creative approach to ingredients and culinary influences from all over the world. While this take on the classic Reuben sandwich with grilled pineapple and a side of red cabbage and pecan coleslaw, found at a Perth food market, may have strayed a long way from its New York ancestor, it's very clearly a new classic in the making.

_____

For the coleslaw, finely slice the red cabbage. Add the salt, vinegar and marmalade and massage until softened. Toss with the olive oil and sesame oil and season with salt and pepper. Add the pecan nuts.

For the sandwiches, peel and slice the red onion. Season with salt and a dash of red wine vinegar. Wash and spin dry the lettuce leaves.

Heat the oil in a large non-stick pan. Add the pineapple slices and fry until golden brown, about 2–3 minutes per side. Sprinkle with a little of the chilli flakes. Pick off the coriander leaves, chop and add to the pineapple.

Preheat the oven using the grill function. Toast the bread on one side only. Spread each bread slice thinly with mustard on the untoasted side. Top 4 with slices of cheese and grill until the cheese has melted, being careful not to let the cheese brown.

Put together 2 sandwiches as shown in the photo. Finish with a slice of bread with melted cheese on top.

Serve immediately with the gherkins and coleslaw. These are best eaten with a knife and fork.

FREMANTLE SARDINE PLATE

Greek style!

We reach the port of Fremantle, once a legendary hang-out for hippies near Perth, early in the morning while it's still dark. Fisherman Jim Mendolia has offered to take us on a sardine fishing trip. Jim and his crew are among the few who still head out to sea almost every day (they take Saturdays off though) to catch sardines along a 600-mile strip of Western Australian coastline. Only a small part of their catch goes straight to restaurants, because he keeps the bulk of it for processing in his small family-run factory, where the fish is cleaned, filleted, marinated and packaged to add value and secure the family's income. The outcome – marinated sardine fillets from Jim Mendolia's Fremantle Sardine Company – are thick, juicy and delicately seasoned. In fact, these are the best sardine fillets I've ever tasted.

We take part of the catch across to the gorgeous Fremantle Fishing Boat Harbour and on to Cicerello's Landing, a fish restaurant that looks very American and is clearly well prepared for customers arriving in mad rushes. Its specialty is fish and chips, which they claim is the best in south-western Australia. We have brought our own sardines, and the Greek owner, a friend of Jim's, fries the fresh catch in his kitchen, seasoned only with oregano and chilli – breakfast straight from a plancha.

HERE'S HOW (serves 4)

Peel and mince **1–2 garlic cloves**. Combine with **8 tbsp olive oil**. Chop **4 sprigs fresh oregano** (or 1 tsp dried). Add together with **chilli flakes** to taste. Cut **3–4 tomatoes** in 8 wedges each, slice **1–2 organic Lebanese cucumbers** thickly and season with salt. Arrange the vegetables on a platter together with 150 g (1 cup) feta. Drizzle with **lemon juice** and 2–3 tbsp of the garlic oil.

Rinse **20 fresh, cleaned small sardines** under cold water. Drain and turn in a little flour. Heat **4–5 tbsp fresh olive oil** in a large non-stick pan over high heat. Add the fish and fry 2–3 minutes each side. Season with salt and drizzle with the remaining garlic oil and a little **lemon juice**. Serve with the salad.

BOTTOMS UP!

This goes well with a juicy South Australian Chardonnay, a light and fruity rosé or a straight lager.

NON-ALCOHOLIC: try lemon water with mint.

TOASTED MACADAMIAS

with shichimi togarashi

Australians love nuts, and the Australian macadamia is the queen of nuts. Macadamias are crunchy, sweet, with a buttery taste – and they are infamously difficult to crack. All this justifies the high price of this exquisite nut, which we combine here with shichimi togarashi, a Japanese seven-spice chilli mix. Its main flavours are chilli, sansho pepper, mandarin peel, poppy seeds, sesame seeds and aonori seaweed. This spice mix is commonly available from Asian stores and the Asian or spice section of well-stocked supermarkets. If you cannot get shichimi togarashi, season to taste with freshly ground black pepper, chilli flakes and a little finely grated orange or mandarin zest.

HERE'S HOW (makes 275 g spiced nuts)

Preheat the oven to 180°C (350°F). Whisk **1 egg white** until stiff with **a little salt** and **a pinch of sugar**. Combine **125 g (¾ cup) macadamia nuts**, **150 g (1 cup) cashews**, **1 tsp shichimi togarashi** and the **juice and finely grated zest of ½ lime** with the egg white. Be measured with the shichimi togarashi, as it's quite spicy! Toss everything and drain the seasoned nuts in a sieve. Transfer to a tray lined with baking paper and dry in the preheated oven for 6 minutes. Remove the baking paper and toast the nuts on the tray for another 6 minutes to brown them all over. Leave the nuts to cool fully to get them perfectly crunchy.

This recipe also works with other types of nuts such as hazelnuts, walnuts or almonds.

MUSIC: *Fat Freddy's Drop, a New Zealand band that combines roots, reggae and dub with a bit of soul, jazz, funk and a pinch of electronica, lifts the mood as the shadows deepen. Recommended listening: their 2013 album "Black Bird".*

BOTTOMS UP!

This nut mix is a new favourite bar food to go with just about anything, but it's particularly nice with sherry Fino, Amontillado or Oloroso.

JAPAN

Japanese cuisine is about the energy and qualities inherent in different foods. It focuses on the product and every detail of its seemingly simple preparation.

Japanese chefs decide on a particular aspect of their cuisine such as sushi, tempura or ramen early in their careers and then dedicate their lives to achieving mastery in their chosen discipline. In this process, carefulness and mindfulness are as important as a deep appreciation of good produce and the hard work of farmers, breeders, fishermen and manufacturers. In Japan, cooking starts with the perfect ingredient, and it is the cook's task to showcase the food optimally.

During a trip to Tokyo, I was able to watch a number of master chefs at work. Japanese restaurants are often tiny, seating maybe a dozen people along a counter behind which the chef and his apprentices work right in front of the guests. Transparency is important, and everybody in the open kitchen moves gently and skilfully in focused silence, interrupted only occasionally by short commands and apprentices' brief replies. Japanese kitchens are impressive displays of skill and teamwork that culminate in the beautiful food they produce.

I ate the best sushi of my life in Japan, prepared by grand master Nagano-san, with airily light grains of warm rice packed gently together, the freshest fish and seafood and complex soups, all with incredible clarity and depth of flavours. Speaking of soups! Fragrant miso soup! Aromatic ramen noodle soups that warm you through and through first thing in the morning – who needs muesli! Master tempura chef Tetsuya Saotome's restaurant was an eye-opener: an entire menu of amazing ingredients, all deep-fried, but cooked so very differently from your standard deep-fried food. His freshly prepared batter produces a myriad of consistencies, viscosities and flavours, enveloping delicate, juicy prawns, melt-in-your-mouth octopus, shiso leaves and sea urchin roe, green asparagus and tasty shiitake mushrooms. The recipes in this chapter reflect the cooking you'll find in izakayas, small bars that serve uncomplicated food (see p. 34) alongside sake, rice spirits and beer.

In Japan, the last light has social meaning. People set off from work together with their colleagues, and bars allows them to dispense with the ever-present strict rules, conventions and hierarchies of Japanese life, even if only for a little while. Yakitori skewers (p. 31) are very popular bar foods. They are grilled over burning coals in open kitchens, with chefs turning them regularly and basting them with their secret yakitori sauce until they are beautifully caramelised. A perfect side dish for cool, silky sake served in traditional wooden sake bowls. Oh, Japan!

MIXED YAKITORI

MIXED YAKITORI (makes 4–6 skewers each)

BASIC YAKITORI SAUCE

Prepare a seasoning sauce from **4 tbsp soy sauce**, **2 tbsp mirin** and **2 tbsp teriyaki sauce**. If you like, add **a little chilli or chilli sauce** for heat.

CHICKEN YAKITORI

Debone **3 chicken thighs** and cut the meat into strips. Marinate in **1 tsp mirin** and **1 tbsp sake**. Trim the fat off **150 g chicken hearts**. Halve and rinse thoroughly under cold water. Pat dry and thread on skewers, alternating with the thigh strips. Fry the skewers in **3 tbsp hot peanut oil** 3–4 minutes on each side. Add the yakitori sauce, leave to bubble up and turn the skewers in the sauce. Serve garnished with **1–2 tbsp freshly sliced spring onion rolls**.

OCTOPUS YAKITORI

Marinate **200 g baby octopus** (fresh, or frozen and defrosted) in **1 tbsp lime juice** and **½ finely minced garlic clove**, then skewer. Fry the skewers in **3 tbsp hot peanut oil** for 3–4 minutes on each side. Add the yakitori sauce, leave to bubble up and turn the skewers in the sauce until they start to caramelise.

ASPARAGUS AND MUSHROOM YAKITORI

Dry-roast **1 tbsp sesame seeds** in a pan. Trim the woody ends off **6–8 spears of green asparagus**. Peel the bottom thirds thinly and cut the spears into thirds. Remove the stems from **6–8 shiitake mushrooms**. Halve the caps and skewer, alternating between the mushrooms and asparagus. Fry the skewers in **3 tbsp hot peanut oil** for 3–4 minutes on each side. Add the yakitori sauce, leave to bubble up and turn the skewers in the sauce. Serve sprinkled with **sesame**.

— KANPAI! —

Japanese food goes well with sake, which is mostly served cool. Bowls are filled to the brim as a sign of hospitality and generosity. Sherry also goes very well with Japanese food, and many izakayas serve beer with it.

NON-ALCOHOLIC: freshly brewed green tea, ginger or herbal lemonade.

MUSIC: *United Future Organization (formerly: U.F.O.), a band founded by Tadashi Yabe, Toshio Matsuura and the Frenchman Raphael Sebbag in 1990, redefined 90s club jazz not only in Japan but also well beyond. All of their records of the time are still perfect bar and club music, especially as the sun goes down. My favourites: "Bon Voyage" (1999) and "3rd Perspective" (1996).*

1 Edamame
2 Mixed yakitori
3 Karaage
4 Negi maguro

EDAMAME, NEGI MAGURO, KARAAGE

EDAMAME (serves 4)

Edamame – fresh soybeans in the pod – served with a sprinkle of sea salt is a classic snack and izakaya bar food. Very easy to make and very delicious.

———

Add **400 g frozen edamame** to boiling water. Return to a boil and simmer for 3–4 minutes. Drain and refresh under cold water. Sprinkle with a little **sea salt** and serve straight away, still wet. To eat, open the pods with gentle pressure and nibble the delicate beans straight from their pods.

NEGI MAGURO (serves 2–4)

Tuna with leek – I first encountered this absolutely delectable tuna recipe in one of my favourite Japanese restaurants in Hamburg, the Akari in Hamburg-Winterhude. This is my DIY attempt; for the original you'll have to eat there!

———

Prepare a seasoning sauce from **1 tbsp soy sauce**, **1 tbsp sweet soy sauce**, **1 tsp mirin** and **3 tbsp dashi stock** (alternatively cold vegetable stock). Divide among 4 bowls. Finely slice **1 spring onion**. Cut **300 g tuna fillet** into about 1 cm dice and divide among 4 other bowls. Sprinkle with the spring onion and serve immediately. Guests dip their fish cubes into the sauce as they eat. Serve with some **wasabi** for heat.

KARAAGE (serves 4)

Marinated chicken, deep-fried until crisp. A perfect accompaniment to sake and beer.

———

Combine **1 tbsp soy sauce**, **2 tbsp sake** and **1 tbsp mirin**. Add a little **sriracha sauce** for heat. Cut **500 g chicken fillet** into pieces 2–3 cm thick and toss with the marinade. Heat **oil** in a deep-fryer according to the manufacturer's instructions; alternatively add about 8 cm oil to a tall saucepan and heat to 170°C (340°F).* Preheat the oven to 80°C (175°F). Turn the chicken pieces in a little **cornflour (cornstarch)**. Shake off excess starch and deep-fry in batches in the hot fat, about 3–5 minutes per batch. Drain on kitchen paper and keep warm on a tray in the oven. Finally, deep-fry a few dry leaves of **flat-leaf parsley** for just a few seconds. Season with **salt** and sprinkle over the chicken pieces for garnish.

For the dipping sauce: Dry-roast **1 tbsp sesame seeds** in a pan and combine with **5 tbsp sweet soy sauce** and **1 tbsp lemon juice**.

* If you do not have a cooking thermometer, test with a wooden spoon: Dip the spoon handle into the hot oil. The temperature is right if small bubbles start to rise.

酒 SAKE

AKITA

YAMAGATA

NIIGATA

KOBE

GIFU

CHINA

Spring rolls are popular all over Asia. The Chinese version,
which is often served as part of Chinese New Year festivities,
is most commonly filled with bean sprouts, cabbage and
carrot strips, vermicelli noodles and minced meat.

SPRING ROLLS

INGREDIENTS

(makes 12 spring rolls)

100 g vermicelli noodles

50 g green cabbage

300 g minced meat

3 tbsp oil

50 g bean sprouts

1 tsp five-spice powder

5 tbsp soy sauce

1 tbsp fish sauce

1 carrot

2 spring onions

Salt

1 tsp cornflour (cornstarch)

**12 sheets spring roll pastry
    (21.5 cm long/wide)**

Oil for deep-frying

Hot sweet chilli sauce

Pour boiling water over the vermicelli and leave to soften. Slice the cabbage very finely. Heat the oil in a frying pan. Fry the minced meat and sliced cabbage until crumbly. Add the beansprouts and continue to fry for another 2 minutes. Dust with five-spice powder, add the soy sauce and fish sauce and remove from the heat.

Drain the vermicelli and cut them shorter with scissors. Peel and coarsely grate the carrot. Slice the spring onion into rings and add to the minced meat mixture together with the vermicelli. Toss everything well to combine and season with salt.

Whisk the cornflour with 1 tbsp water. Set out the pastry sheets in front of you, corners pointing towards your body. Divide the filling among the bottom thirds of the sheets and fold the bottom corner over the filling. Fold the two outer corners towards the middle and roll the pastry up towards the upper corner. Moisten the tips with the cornflour water and roll up fully.

Heat oil to 180°C (350°F) in a deep fryer according to the manufacturers' instructions. Alternatively heat the oil in a small, tall saucepan. Deep-fry the spring rolls in the hot oil in batches until golden brown, about 2–3 minutes per batch. Drain on kitchen paper and serve with hot sweet chilli sauce.

* If you do not have a cooking thermometer, test with a wooden spoon: Dip the spoon handle into the hot oil. The temperature is right if small bubbles start to rise.

GANBEI!

Have these spring rolls with Chinese Tsingtao beer or with the exquisite (and pricey) Maotai, a sweet and bitter fermented spirit made of millet and wheat, which is traditionally served in miniature glasses and always downed in shots.

BAOZI

Steamed yeast buns with braised meat

INGREDIENTS

(makes 12 baozi)

For the filling:

1 kg pork belly, with rind

20 g ginger

2 garlic cloves

**50 ml (2½ tbsp) shaoxing cooking wine
(alternatively Oloroso sherry)**

1 tsp five-spice powder

1 tsp fennel seeds

1 tsp raw sugar

Salt

80 ml (5 tbsp) soy sauce

For the baozi:

8 g fresh yeast

1 tbsp sugar

130 ml (½ cup) water

260 g (1 cup) flour (type 405)

1 tsp baking powder

Salt

1 tbsp oil

1 drop sesame oil

2–3 spring onions

The pork belly for filling these fluffy, soft steamed buns is marinated in spices overnight and then slowly braised until completely soft the next day. Heed Confucius's wisdom, who knew that guests should always wait for freshly steamed buns, never the other way around!

For the filling, on the day before serving, trim the rind off the pork belly. Reserve the rind. Peel and mince the ginger and garlic. Combine the wine, five-spice powder, fennel, ginger, garlic, sugar and ½ tsp salt to a marinade. Rub the marinade into the meat. Cover and marinate in the refrigerator overnight.

The next day, remove the meat from the marinade and pat dry. Reserve the marinade. Score the rind several times with a sharp knife. Transfer to a hot frying pan and render until the bottom of the pan is covered lightly with oil. Remove the pork rind. Add the meat and brown all over. Transfer the browned meat to a saucepan. Add the marinade, soy sauce and 1 litre of water. Cover and braise for 1 hour. Remove the lid and continue to braise for another hour, turning occasionally.

Meanwhile, for the baozi, dissolve the yeast and sugar in water. Combine the flour, baking powder and a pinch of salt in the bowl of a food processor fitted with dough hooks. Add the yeast mixture and two types of oil. Combine and knead to a smooth dough. Continue to knead at low speed until pliable, about 10 minutes. This can also be done manually or with the dough hook of an electric mixer. Shape the dough into a ball. Cover with a clean dish towel and leave to rise for 30 minutes.

Divide the dough into 12 pieces. Dust your hands with flour and shape the pieces into smooth balls, folding the dough in on itself. Cover the dough balls and leave to rise for another 30 minutes.

Remove the pork from its gravy. Use two forks to pull the meat into shreds and a knife to cut the shreds into small pieces. Return to the gravy. Shape the dough balls into flat rounds. Place about 1 tablespoon of the filling into the centre of each piece. Fold the dough together on top of the filling and press to seal well.

Fill a saucepan (with a lid and steamer insert) with 1 litre water. Bring to a boil. Line the steamer insert with baking paper. Place half of the baozi onto the steamer, seam side down, cover and steam for 8 minutes. Slice the spring onions into rings. Serve the steamed baozi garnished with the spring onions, then prepare the second batch. Serve the remaining braised meat with the baozi.

WONTON SOUP

INGREDIENTS

(serves 4)

1 fresh whole chicken

2 chicken thighs

25 g ginger

3 garlic cloves

Light soy sauce

1 bunch soup vegetables

2 onions

4 sticks lemongrass

2 l (8 cups) chicken stock

50 ml (2½ tbsp) sweet soy sauce

2 tsp sugar

300 g chicken hearts

Salt

1 bunch spring onions

**1 packet frozen wonton wrappers
(or 20 fresh wrappers)**

This is a very sophisticated, yet easily prepared version of a classic Chinese snack of delicate dumplings in a fragrant broth.

Coarsely chop the fresh whole chicken. Debone the chicken thighs, reserving the bones. Dice the deboned thighs. Toss with the grated ginger, 1 minced clove garlic and 2 tbsp soy sauce. Cover and set aside to marinate.

Peel, wash and coarsely dice the soup vegetables. Halve the onions, leaving them unpeeled. Crush 2 garlic cloves and pound the lemongrass with the back of a heavy kitchen knife. Add everything to a saucepan together with the chicken stock, 50 ml soy sauce and the sugar and bring to a boil. Trim the

fat off the chicken hearts. Halve and rinse thoroughly in lukewarm water. Add the whole chicken, reserved bones and chicken hearts to the boiling stock. Season and simmer, uncovered, for 90 minutes over low heat.

For the wontons, lightly salt the marinated chicken thighs and grind them in a mixer or food processor together with the marinade and 1 coarsely chopped spring onion. Soak a dish towel in hot water and place it on the stacked frozen wonton wrappers, if using. The first wrapper will soon be defrosted without you needing to defrost the whole lot, which you can then refreeze for another use.

Remove 20 wrappers in total. Place 1 teaspoon of the filling in the centre of each wrapper. Moisten the edges with water and fold to seal. Use 2 teaspoons to shape the remaining filling into small balls.

Strain the chicken stock through a sieve. Cook the wontons and meatballs in boiling salted water for 6 minutes. Season the chicken stock with salt. Slice the remaining spring onions into rings, add and return to a boil. Strain the wontons and meatballs and serve in soup bowls in the broth.

TIP: For an even more aromatic broth, leave the stock overnight to allow the flavours to develop. Strain the next day. If you like, return the chicken hearts to the strained broth and serve in the soup. They are delicate and delicious, and while heart is considered offal, it is in fact pure muscle meat.

CHINESE SPRING ONION PANCAKES

INGREDIENTS

(makes 12 pancakes)

360 g (1½ cups) flour (type 405,
    plus extra for dusting)

1 level tsp baking powder

Salt

220 ml (7½ fl oz) warm water

1–2 drops sesame oil

4 spring onions

Oil for frying

6 tbsp soy sauce

4 tbsp hot sweet chilli sauce

3 tbsp rice vinegar

Combine the flour, baking powder and a little salt in the bowl of a food processor fitted with dough hooks. Add the warm water. Combine and knead to a smooth dough. Continue to knead at low speed until pliable, about 5 minutes. This can also be done manually or with the dough hook of an electric mixer. Shape the dough into a ball. Brush thinly with sesame oil, cover with a clean dish towel and leave to rest for 30 minutes.

Divide the dough into 12 even pieces and shape into balls. Dust your work surface with flour and roll out the balls into thin rounds. Slice the spring onions finely, season lightly with salt and divide among the dough rounds. Roll up the dough and shape the rolls into snails. Roll out the snails into thin rounds again.

Preheat the oven to 80°C (175°F). Heat a little oil in a large non-stick pan and fry the pancakes until golden brown, about 3–4 minutes per side. Keep the cooked pancakes warm in the oven. Slice and serve with dipping sauce.

For the dipping sauce: Combine the soy sauce, chilli sauce and rice vinegar and serve with the pancakes.

MUSIC: *Chinese Man is a French music project whose founders, Zé Mateo, SLY and High Ku, collaborate with various artists to create music that fuses trip hop and jazz grooves with hip-hop and sampled world music. Their 2009 album "The Groove Sessions, Vol. 2" is just perfect for the sunset.*

INDIA

Indian cuisine is full of colour and a myriad of aromas.
This comforting, spicy food is the product of the
multitude of religious and cultural influences that
make up the peoples of India.

PANEER CIGAR ROLLS

VEGETABLE PAKORAS WITH MINT YOGHURT

PANEER CIGAR ROLLS (makes 12 cigars)

Paneer cigar rolls are deep-fried pastry rolls filled with a mixture of unsalted Indian paneer cheese, which has been replaced by a feta and ricotta mixture here. This detracts in no way from the delight that are these crisp cigars, quite the contrary: this fusion of Indian, Greek and Italian influences has spades of flavour!

———

Finely slice **6 mint leaves, 2 sprigs coriander (cilantro)** and **red chilli** to taste. Combine with **100 g (⅔ cup) crumbled feta** and **100 g (½ cup) ricotta**. Whisk **1 tsp cornflour (cornstarch)** with **1 tbsp water**. Set out **12 spring roll pastry sheets (21.5 cm long/wide)** in front of you, corners pointing towards your body. Divide the filling among the pastry, fold the two outer corners towards the middle and roll the pastry up towards the upper corner. Moisten the tips with the cornflour water and roll up fully. Deep-fry the cigars in **plenty of oil** at 180°C (350°F). Do this in batches, about 4–6 minutes each.

VEGETABLE PAKORAS (makes 12 pakoras)

Colourful vegetables and chickpeas, seasoned with garam masala and deep-fried in a chickpea batter. Served with mint yoghurt, these are highly addictive. Lucky these pakoras are so easy to make.

———

Combine **200 g (1⅔ cups) besan flour** with **1 tsp baking powder** and ½ tsp garam masala. Add **200 ml (¾ cup) water** and the **juice of ½ lime** and whisk to a smooth, pancake-like batter. Season with **salt**. Finely slice **100 g green cabbage leaves**. Finely dice **100 g broccoli** and **1 red capsicum**. Mince **½–1 green chilli** and **4 sprigs coriander**. Add to the batter together with **2 tbsp raisins** and **100 g drained chickpeas (⅝ cup)** from a tin. Heat a generous amount of **ghee** in a large frying pan. Shape tablespoon-sized pakoras and fry, for around 3–4 minutes each.

Stir **4–6 mint leaves**, finely chopped, into **250 g yoghurt** and season with a little salt. Optionally sprinkle with **toasted black sesame seeds** and **chilli flakes** and serve with the pakoras.

MUSIC: *Leeds band Black Star Liner mix heavy dub and dance with Indian sounds such as tabla drums, sitar and shenai. A great example is their 1999 album "Bengali Bantam Youth Experience".*

1 Paneer cigar rolls
2 Vegetable pakoras with mint yoghurt
3 Samosas
4 Tandoori chicken

LENTIL & SPINACH SAMOSAS

TANDOORI CHICKEN

SAMOSAS (makes 8 samosas)

This recipe is a traditional Indian way of using leftovers, with samosas often filled with the remnants of yesterday's feast. This recipe uses freshly cooked ingredients though, with a crisp pastry encasing a juicy spinach and curried lentil filling.

———

Cook **60 g red lentils (⅓ cup)** with **1 tsp curry powder** in **250 ml (1 cup) water** until soft, about 6–8 minutes. Set aside to cool in a sieve. Peel **1 onion** and **1 garlic clove**. Mince the garlic and finely dice the onion. Heat **1 tbsp ghee** in a frying pan. Add the onion and garlic and fry until translucent. Add **200 g spinach** and leave to wilt. Season with **salt**. Transfer to a plate to cool. Combine all ingredients with **50 g crumbled feta (⅓ cup)** and season with salt. Preheat the oven to 220°C (430°F). Cut **8 large filo or yufka pastry sheets** into thirds. Brush thinly with **oil** and layer three pastry pieces each on top of each other (8 x 3 pieces). Divide the mixture for the filling into eight portions. Place one portion each on the bottom right of the pastry pieces. Fold the pastry over the filling to make a neat triangle encasing the filling. Keep folding the triangle over and to the side until you reach the end of the pastry strip and have a well-sealed pastry parcel. Transfer the pastries to a tray lined with baking paper and bake in the preheated oven for 10 minutes.

TANDOORI CHICKEN (serves 4)

Indian tandoori spice paste (tandoori masala) once got its intensely red colour from genuine saffron. These days, it usually has added food colouring, but the flavour remains incomparable. In India, tandoori chicken is cooked on skewers in tandoors, charcoal-fired clay ovens.

———

Preheat the oven to 200°C (390°F). Pierce **8 chicken thighs** all over with the tip of a sharp knife. Whisk **4 tbsp tandoori paste** with **2 tbsp yoghurt** and **1 tsp oil** until smooth and rub the mixture into the chicken. Transfer to the preheated oven and cook in about 35–40 minutes. Season with salt and serve garnished with **fresh slices of red onion**.

COLOURS,
FLAVOURS, AROMAS
– THAT'S INDIA!

TURKEY

One of the most beautiful vegetable dishes of Turkish cuisine:
the original consists of eggplants stuffed with onions and
tomatoes and slowly braised in plenty of olive oil in the oven.
There are numerous variations of this dish, using rice,
pine nuts and capsicum, among others.

İMAM BAYILDI

Swooning imam

INGREDIENTS

(serves 4)

1 zucchini (courgette)

Salt

1 eggplant (aubergine)

Olive oil

Freshly ground black pepper

1 tin diced tomatoes
   (425 g net weight)

1 garlic clove

1 sprig each thyme and oregano

1 tsp sugar

½–1 red chilli

150 g (1¼ cup) feta

A few leaves of flat-leaf parsley

Legend has it that an honourable imam fainted in view of the very generous quantities of olive oil used in these stuffed eggplants. This dish makes a perfect main course, but is also great served cold as part of a *mezze* platter for the day's last rays.

———

Slice the zucchini lengthwise into about 12 thin strips. Arrange the strips on a baking tray in a single layer, sprinkle with salt and set aside for 30 minutes. Slice the eggplant lengthwise, also into 12 thin strips. Heat a large saucepan and fry the strips until golden brown in batches of 5–6 slices each, using 6–8 tbsp of olive oil per batch. Season with salt and pepper.

Bring the tomatoes to a boil in a saucepan together with 2 tbsp olive oil, the minced garlic, herbs, sugar and chilli (split open). Simmer gently to reduce for about 15 minutes. Season with salt.

Meanwhile, pat the zucchini dry with kitchen paper and top each slice with 1 slice of eggplant. Finely crumble the feta and divide among the vegetable slices. Roll up.

Remove the chilli, thyme and oregano from the reduced tomato sauce. Transfer the sauce to a heatproof dish and stand the vegetable rolls inside the sauce. Cook in the preheated oven (220°C / 430°F; best avoid using the fan-forced function) on the second rack from the bottom for 10 minutes. Serve garnished with parsley leaves.

EAT WITH: Rice, bulgur or couscous.

MUSIC: *The Turkish band BaBa ZuLa from Istanbul merges Anatolian folk and Oriental tunes with rock, reggae and dub elements – a truly magic combination! Recommended listening: their 2017 double album "XX", released to celebrate the band's 20th anniversary.*

CHICKEN DONER KEBAB WITH CACIK

INGREDIENTS

(serves 4)

For the doner kebab:

2 chicken breasts, with skin

Olive oil

2 pinches baking soda

4 sprigs oregano, chopped
   (or ½ tsp dried oregano)

2 pinches freshly grated
   organic lemon zest

Pul biber (chilli flakes)

1 red onion

Dash of herb vinegar

Salt

4 red bullhorn capsicums (peppers)

4 mini pita breads

A few leaves flat-leaf parsley

For the cabbage salad:

400 g green cabbage

Salt

1–2 tbsp herb vinegar

1 tsp walnut oil

1 tbsp olive oil

For the cacık:

1–2 organic Lebanese cucumbers

Salt

1 garlic clove

300 g (1¼ cups) Greek yoghurt

1 tbsp olive oil

1 bunch dill, finely chopped

Doner kebabs were actually created in Berlin: stuffing pita bread with juicy, grilled kebab meat and sides is entirely alien to traditional Turkish cuisine. But then Kadir Nurman, a Turkish migrant, came up with what was to become Berlin's unofficial trademark dish, the doner kebab, in 1972, and his invention spread throughout Germany and beyond in no time. Early on, Nurman, who died in 2013, aged 80, sold this novel food from his stand at Berlin Zoo station for a mere 1.50 marks (a little over a dollar). He later somewhat regretted that he never thought to protect his culinary invention, but he was also delighted that his compatriots were able to do such good business with it and that millions of people came to love "his" doner kebab.

———

Remove the skin from the chicken breasts. Slice the skin into thin strips. Refrigerate. Cut the meat into bite-sized pieces, and toss with 2 tbsp olive oil and the baking soda, oregano, lemon zest and chilli flakes to taste. Refrigerate.

For the cabbage salad, remove the cabbage's core and slice into very fine strips. Season. Add the herb vinegar, walnut and olive oils and massage until softened.

For the cacık, finely dice the cucumber and sprinkle with salt. Peel and mince the garlic. Combine with the cucumber, yoghurt, olive oil and dill. Season with salt.

Peel the onion and slice into fine rings. Season with herb vinegar and salt. Set aside. Quarter and deseed the capsicums and sprinkle lightly with salt. Heat 4 tbsp olive oil in a frying pan over medium heat and fry the capsicums for 8–12 minutes. Remove from the pan and keep warm. Add another 1 tbsp olive oil to the pan and fry the chicken skin strips until crisp. Remove and keep warm. Reheat the pan over high heat. Add the chicken mixture and fry until golden brown, about 6–8 minutes. Season with salt and toss in the crisp chicken skin.

Halve the pita breads and briefly warm them under the grill (broiler) or in a toaster. Spread the bottoms with the cacık, fill with the capsicum, chicken, cabbage salad, onion rings and a little parsley. Cover with the tops.

BAKLAVA

Cevizli baklava

INGREDIENTS

(serves 12–18)

1 cinnamon stick

2 bay leaves

2 star anise

4 cloves

500 g (2¼ cups) sugar

4 tbsp lemon juice

Zest of 1 organic orange,
    finely grated

350 g (3 cups) walnut kernels

50 g (½ cup) green pistachio
    kernels, chopped

250 g (1 cup) butter

300 g filo or yufka pastry sheets

Baklava is thin sheets of filo or yufka pastry layered with a richly spiced nut and syrup mixture. This type of sweet is very popular throughout the Middle East and south-eastern Europe, but recipes vary widely, using different ingredients and spices. Turkish baklava, called cevizli baklava, is traditionally made with walnuts and pistachios. Cutting the originally round cake into the classic diamond shapes is a science in itself, but luckily looks don't affect the taste!

———

Add the cinnamon stick, bay leaves, star anise and cloves, sugar and 750 ml (3 cups) water to a saucepan and boil for 10 minutes to make a syrup. Season with lemon juice and orange zest and set aside to cool fully. Remove the spices.

Meanwhile, chop the walnuts in a mixer and combine them with the chopped pistachios. Set aside 2 tbsp of the mixture for garnish. Melt the butter. Brush a springform tin (approx. 28 cm Ø) thinly with butter, cover with a sheet of filo pastry and brush again thinly with butter.

Repeat with another pastry sheet, pushing the pastry together somewhat to create little folds for a particularly light baklava. Do this also for the remaining sheets. Cover the tin with alternating layers of 2–3 sheets filo pastry and the nut mixture until all ingredients have been used up. Finish with 2 sheets of pastry and pour over the remaining butter.

Preheat the oven to 160°C (320°F). Before baking, use a very sharp knife to cut the baklava in the tin into diamond, square or rectangular shapes. Bake in the preheated oven until golden brown, about 40 minutes.

Remove the baklava from the oven. Drizzle generously with the cooled syrup while still hot. Sprinkle with the remaining nuts, leave to cool fully and serve.

ĐEREFE!

Baklava is best eaten with black tea or a strong coffee.

GREECE

Greek cuisine is so much more than meat and rice eaten
with a generous side of blue-and-white sirtaki folk kitsch –
an insight that has started to spread around the world.

The idea that Greek cuisine has a heavy focus on meat is a misunderstanding from the 70s, when Greek migrants thought they should adapt their cuisine to their richer host countries, especially Germany, where people were very fond of meat. Traditional Greek cooking, in contrast, is much more focused on vegetables. In fact, Greek Orthodox Christians eat a vegetarian diet for about four months a year due to various religious fasting requirements.

Another misunderstanding concerns ouzo, which is not served as a digestif in Greece but is rather a cultural fixture with deep roots in Greek culinary life. Greeks drink ouzo whenever they have time – time for a few mezze bites, time for friends and family, time for talking and enjoying life. As a rule, generosity is of the essence when sharing ouzo. Avoid anything that costs less than six euros per bottle, and if you're prepared to spend ten or more, things start to get exciting. High-quality ouzo is a true delight, and it is well worthwhile to try a good ouzo at room temperature, as the complex layers of an outstanding product are easily lost when it is served chilled.

Greeks enjoy ouzo with finger foods such as various dips (p. 61), stuffed vine leaves (p. 58) or baked butter beans (p. 64). Greek salad (p. 63) is another classic that is often tampered with to its detriment. Yet all it takes for a good salad is high-quality vegetables, fragrant herbs, a little vinegar and the best olive oil you can find. At sunset, why not serve it with feta saganaki or feta in butter (p. 63), a sophisticated recipe from contemporary Greek cuisine.

Greek wine too has evolved. The times of overly resinated, headache-inducing retsinas have long gone, and a young, dedicated generation of winemakers has ensured that Greece is currently Europe's most underrated wine country. Greece has Europe's oldest vines, whose grapes form the basis for outstanding wines, some very light, some with a purist mineral character, others powerfully aromatic. It's definitely worthwhile doing a little research online or with a reputable wine dealer – or just ask the chef at your favourite Greek restaurant. Then try out your newly discovered wines at sunset, the sky pink and orange, and dream of your next Greek holiday over the fabulous Greek recipes below. What was it again that Demis Roussos sang about back in the days… *"Strawberries, cherries and an angel's kiss in spring, My summer wine is really made from all these things."*

STUFFED VINE LEAVES

INGREDIENTS

(makes 30–35 stuffed vine leaves)

1 jar or tin of vine leaves (approx. 400 g)

25 g (3 tbsp) pine nuts

2 onions

3 tbsp olive oil

150 g (¾ cup) long-grain rice

50 g (¼ cup) raisins

1 tbsp tomato paste

Ground cinnamon

1 pinch allspice

1 tsp dried mint (optional)

Salt

500 ml (2 cups) strong vegetable stock

1 bunch flat-leaf parsley

4 sprigs dill

Lemon juice

Dolmades, a true classic of Greek cooking, do require a little effort and skill (unless you're Greek, of course). However, the effort pays off in these delicately braised vine leaves, stuffed with moist spiced rice, pine nuts, herbs and raisins. Serve lukewarm as a fabulous snack for a Greek sunset!

———

Unfold and separate the vine leaves. Transfer to a bowl and scald with boiling water. Set aside. Dry-roast the pine nuts in a pan until golden brown. Peel and finely dice the onions. Add the olive oil and onions to the pine nuts and sauté until the onions are soft.

Add the rice and raisins and stir in the tomato paste. Season with a pinch of cinnamon, allspice, dried mint and salt. Ladle in the stock and simmer, uncovered, for 10 minutes. Remove from the heat, cover and set aside to absorb all of the liquid. Transfer the rice to a cutting board or plate to cool. Finely chop the parsley and dill and combine with the cooled rice. Drizzle with a little lemon juice and check the seasoning.

Remove the softened vine leaves from the water. Trim off the hard stems and spread the leaves on a clean dish towel with the shiny side facing down. Place about 1 tsp of the rice mixture onto the lower half of each leaf. Fold in the sides and roll the leaf up tightly. Continue until the mixture is used up (makes about 30–35 rolls).

Line a deep pan or shallow saucepan with the remaining vine leaves. Cover with the stuffed vine leaves, tightly packed. Weigh down with a plate that fits inside the pan or saucepan and pour in enough boiling water to cover the stuffed vine leaves. Simmer gently over medium heat for about 45 minutes. Add more boiling water if necessary. Leave to cool in the pan or saucepan and enjoy warm or cold.

SERVE WITH: Lightly salted yoghurt and fresh lemon wedges.

— YAMAS! —

Ouzo on ice with a little water is a good choice.

NON-ALCOHOLIC: chilled green grape juice on ice, flavoured with lemon and a little fresh mint.

OUZO WITH THREE DIPS

A carefully distilled ouzo is an irresistible, highly aromatic delight with hints of aniseed, nutmeg, liquorice and fresh dill. Served pure, Greeks call it "sketo"; served with water, it's "me nero", and if they're after the room temperature version with ice cubes on the side, they ask for "me parakia". Whatever you prefer. In Greece, ouzo is commonly available in 200 ml bottles, including in restaurants – just the right quantity for two drinks each for two happy customers. Ouzo is always, always, always served with at least olives and bread. All set for the evening!

TARAMOSALATA (serves 4–6)

Purée 150 g smoked salmon, 50 g trout caviar, 1 slice white bread (crust removed) and **80 g (⅓ cup) mayonnaise** in a blender to make a smooth cream. Season lightly with **salt** and a little **lemon juice** to taste. Serve garnished with **50 g trout caviar**.

TZATZIKI (serves 4–6)

Coarsely grate 1 organic cucumber, unpeeled, sprinkle with **salt** and set aside. Finely chop **4–6 sprigs dill**. Peel and mince **1 garlic clove**. Combine everything with **250 g (1 cup) Greek yoghurt** and **2 tbsp olive oil**. Season with salt and a dash of **herb vinegar**.

MELITZANOSALATA (serves 4–6)

Prick the skins of 3 eggplants (aubergines) with a fork all over and transfer the eggplants to a baking tray. Cook in the preheated oven (220°C / 430°F) for 45 minutes. Remove, halve and set aside to cool. Scrape out the soft flesh and chop finely. Stir in **50 g (3 tbsp) tahini, 1 tbsp olive oil** and **1 minced garlic clove** and whisk until smooth. Season with a touch of **smoked paprika powder, 1 pinch ground cumin,** a **dash** of **lemon juice** and **salt. Chop 4 sprigs parsley** and **4 mint leaves** and stir in.

MUSIC: *Imam Baildi, an Athens band, plays rembetiko, the traditional blues of Greek underdogs, overlaid with fat hip-hop beats, bouncy swing from the 30s and a generous pinch of gypsy brass. Recommended listening: "The Imam Baildi Cookbook" (2010).*

GREEK SALAD WITH FETA SAGANAKI AND FETA IN BUTTER

GREEK SALAD (serves 4)

Often copied, rarely mastered, but presented here at its best: use the best-quality vegetables you can find, good red wine vinegar and good olive oil. Add basil, dill and fennel greens for extra flavour, and delicious can be that easy!

———

Slice **3 tomatoes (your favourite varieties)** and sprinkle lightly with salt. Finely slice **1 organic cucumber** and also **salt** lightly. Finely chop **60 g fennel** including the fennel greens. Finely chop **2 sprigs dill**. Slice **1 each green and red bullhorn capsicum**. Arrange all salad ingredients on plates or a platter and salt lightly. Garnish with a **handful** of **basil leaves** and **kalamata olives**. Drizzle with **3–4 tbsp red wine vinegar** and **6–8 tbsp olive oil**.

FETA SAGANAKI (serves 2–4)

Feta saganaki means fried feta, regardless of whether it comes inside a batter, with just a dusting of flour or breadcrumbs.

———

Halve **200 g (1½ cups) feta**, halve the two pieces again lengthwise and turn in **2 tbsp flour**. Whisk **1 (medium-sized) egg** and turn the floured feta first in the egg and then in **6 tbsp breadcrumbs**. Gently press the breading in. Important: leave to rest for 30 minutes so that the crumbing dries a little and becomes denser. This makes it crisp up better when frying. Heat a generous amount of **oil** in a large frying pan and fry the feta until golden brown, about 2–4 minutes. Drain on kitchen paper; do not salt.

FETA IN BUTTER (serves 4)

Meltingly soft feta in aromatic paprika and thyme butter. The original recipe is from the restaurant Das Dionysos in Hamburg – thank you Michalis and Gilmas for the inspiration!

———

Preheat the oven to 220°C (430°F). Halve **200 g (1½ cups) feta** and halve the two pieces again lengthwise. Place the feta slices in an ovenproof dish. Peel and finely slice **1 garlic clove**. Melt **50 g (3½ tbsp) butter** in a saucepan. Add the garlic, **1 tsp paprika powder** and **2 sprigs thyme**. Stir in **1 tbsp mild ajvar capsicum paste** and pour the mixture over the feta. Bake in the preheated oven for 15 minutes.

GIGANTES PLAKI

Baked beans Greek style!

INGREDIENTS

(serves 4)

2 onions

1 garlic clove

4 tbsp olive oil

1 tsp raw sugar

1 tsp tomato paste

1 bay leaf

4 sprigs fresh marjoram

½ tsp dried oregano

1 tin butter beans
    (425 g net weight)

1 tin diced tomatoes
    (425 g net weight)

100 ml (½ cup) vegetable stock

2 tbsp mild ajvar capsicum
    (red pepper) paste

Salt

A crunchy crust hides butter-soft beans in a rich tomato sauce seasoned with capsicum and a touch of garlic. Gigantic! This dish also makes an excellent accompaniment to BBQ meat or fish, or simply served with pita bread, feta and fresh onions.

————

Preheat the oven to 220°C (430°F). Peel and finely dice the onions; peel and mince the garlic. Heat the olive oil in a saucepan and sauté both until soft, about 4–6 minutes. Add the sugar and stir to dissolve. Stir the tomato paste into the softened onions.

Add the bay leaf, marjoram and oregano. Drain the beans and toss with the sauce. Stir in the diced tomatoes, stock and ajvar. Season with salt and simmer, uncovered, for 3 minutes. Transfer to an ovenproof dish and bake in the preheated oven for 20–25 minutes.

— YAMAS! —

Ouzo on ice with a little water is a good choice that really takes these beans to a different level.

NON-ALCOHOLIC: try chilled cucumber juice on ice, made of a finely blended, strained cucumber seasoned with a touch of salt and a little fresh mint.

HUNGARY

Hungary was where I first fell head over heels in love,
on holidays, of course. I was probably seven or eight,
and she was a waitress in our hotel.

We spent hot summer days on Lake Balaton, and I took grainy sepia-coloured pictures of my parents and little sister with my brand-new pocket camera. In the evenings, the love of my life served us crisp schnitzels and sweet pancakes in the hotel's large dining hall. Every night! I decided that when I grew up I would return to marry her.

And I did return to Hungary, decades later, having matured just a little, but this time for a very different folly: I ran the Budapest marathon! However, I finished in such a slow time and in such agonising pain that I have referred to this run as "the shame of Budapest" in my personal sporting history ever since. A photo of me at the finish shows me staggering across the line, my face contorted with pain, behind a woman of about seventy with her arms triumphantly and happily raised.

I had trained for the run, but the key to my failure was my curiosity about Hungarian cuisine. The evening before the race, I ate late and plenty: buttered pasta with mounds of toasted breadcrumbs as a side to fiery *bográcsgulyás*, whose spiciness we balanced with generous amounts of red wines by the famous Hungarian winemakers József Bock and Attila Gere. That was after an entrée platter of sausages and pickled vegetables,

and before dessert with sweet walnut pancakes and an apricot schnapps for drinking on next day's marathon, *egészségedre*! Our friendly host wrapped a pair of *kolbász* in newspaper for each of us to take home – spicy, smoked paprika sausages that he told us to enjoy back home. Anybody who has ever been to a Hungarian restaurant knows that they serve very generous portions. That was also the night when I learned about the difference between goulash and *pörkölt* (p. 72) and that a seemingly harmless tiny, light green pepper on the side of the plate can in fact be hotter than any red chilli. I wept and coughed for minutes at the table until the waiters, concerned about my welfare, brought me a glass of milk.

My most recent visit to Hungary was for the Sziget music festival, which comprises a "Hungarian village" within the site, where I ate what has probably been the best goulash soup of my life, together with *csurgatós kenyér*, bread topped with onion and fresh capsicum and drizzled with rendered bacon fat. There were also young Hungarian winemakers in the village, who proudly poured their excellent, full-bodied wines. After the third glass, I thought I saw the beautiful waitress from Lake Balaton. Astonished, I waved at her, but she had already vanished again among the crowd. And really, who am I kidding?

WARM & SPICY: HUNGARIAN HOSPITALITY

SUNSET WITH A VIEW

Not only for romantics: Budapest's historical castle district with the Fisherman's Bastion is the perfect spot for experiencing a spectacular sunset, including a panoramic view of the city in the day's last rays of light. The Bastion is easily reached with the historical Sikló funicular.

THE WORLD'S
MOST TENDER PÖRKÖLT

INGREDIENTS

(serves 6)

1.8 kg beef shank in slices

1 kg mild onions

1–2 garlic cloves

2 tbsp sweet paprika powder

1 tsp hot paprika powder

1 tbsp tomato paste

1 tsp sugar

½ tsp caraway seeds

2 bay leaves

300 ml (1¼ cup) red wine
   (e.g. a light pinot noir)

Ghee

1 red capsicum (pepper)

2 tomatoes

250 ml (1 cup) beef stock

Salt

A few pearl onions and gherkins

200 g (¾ cup) sour cream

A little milk

A few sprigs of dill

EGÉSZSÉGEDRE!

Pörkölt tastes best with the same red wine you use in the cooking: ideally a Kékfrankos (Blaufränkisch) wine from the Hungarian Balaton region, or a light, young pinot noir. Have the red wine lightly chilled at about 16–18°C (60-65°F).

NON-ALCOHOLIC: seasoned tomato juice or lightly salted yoghurt thinned with a little water (e.g. ayran).

Gulyás (Hungarian for shepherd) is the national dish of the Magyars. The word once meant cooked and dried meat, which shepherds used to carry as they walked the country. This later became goulash, traditionally a stew made of lamb, pork and/or chicken with onions, capsicum and diced potatoes. Pörkölt, in contrast, is a dish of beef slowly braised with onions and capsicums in a thick gravy. It is, however, often mistakenly described as goulash. Pörkölt turns out particularly tender if you use meat from the shank instead of classic topside or silverside for this dish, that is the cut that is otherwise generally used for osso buco. This is a meaty yet butter-soft cut that makes a tender, rich pörkölt that will delight your guests.

———

Remove the silver skin around the beef shank slices. Trim the meat off the bone and cut into bite-sized pieces. Reserve the bones and set aside. Scoop the marrow from the bones and melt in a casserole dish over medium heat. Peel and halve the onions and slice finely. Peel and mince the garlic. Fry the onions in the marrow until light brown. Dust with paprika powder and stir in the tomato paste and sugar. Add the garlic, caraway and bay leaves. Deglaze with red wine, bring to a boil and simmer, uncovered, for 2 minutes. Set aside.

Heat a little ghee in a non-stick pan over high heat. Sear the diced meat in batches, then transfer to the casserole dish. Quarter the capsicum, deseed and dice. Dice the tomatoes and stir both vegetables into the meat mixture. Add the stock and bones. Cover and braise gently over low heat for 2 hours, stirring occasionally. Season with salt.

Finely dice the pickles. Whisk the sour cream and milk until creamy and season with a little salt. Pick off the dill leaves. Remove the bones and bay leaves from the casserole dish and serve the pörkölt with the pickles, sour cream and dill.

PICKLED CAPSICUM WITH SALAMI BAGUETTE

INGREDIENTS

(serves 4–6)

500 g red, yellow and green
    mini capsicums (peppers)

Salt

4 sprigs dill

4 sprigs tarragon

1 garlic clove

150 ml (1¼ cups) white wine
    vinegar

80 g (6 tbsp) sugar

1 tsp mustard seeds

½ tsp caraway

1 bay leaf

Hungarian salami

White bread stick

Spicy Hungarian salami is famous all over the world. It's particularly good served with sweet and sour pickled capsicums on white, crusty bread: a real treat at the end of the day.

———

Remove the stems from the capsicums. Boil the capsicums in salted water for 10 minutes, then drain. Layer them in a pickling jar while still hot, together with the dill and tarragon.

Peel and finely slice the garlic. Combine 150 ml (1¼ cups) water with the garlic, vinegar, sugar, mustard seeds, caraway, bay leaf and 5 g salt in a small saucepan. Bring to a boil. Simmer for 1 minute and pour hot over the capsicums. Leave to cool, seal and store in the refrigerator. These pickled capsicums taste best after a few days. Refrigerated, they will keep for up to 14 days, but they don't usually make it that long. Especially if you have them with salami on white, crusty bread.

MUSIC: *The Budapest band Fran Palermo serve casually sophisticated indie pop with a pinch of folk, rock and electronica on their eponymous 2015 album – all delivered with cheerful lightness.*

— EGÉSZSÉGEDRE! —

Have this with a glass of red, alternatively with a well-chilled *Tokaji* wine from the Tokaj-Hegyalja region. These sweet wines made of yellow Muscat, *Hárslevelű* and Furmint grapes harmonise very well with the spiciness of the rich salami and the sweet and sour capsicums.

NON-ALCOHOLIC: chilled green grape juice, mixed with verjus in a ratio of 2:1.

SAUERKRAUT PUFF PASTRY POCKETS

INGREDIENTS

(makes 24 pockets)

1 packet of puff pastry, frozen
   (1 kg/6 sheets)

500 g (3⅓ cups) sauerkraut

1 mild onion

1 garlic clove

Ghee for frying

250 g minced meat of choice

½ tsp caraway

1 tbsp sweet paprika powder

½ tsp hot paprika powder

5 sprigs marjoram (alternatively
   ½ tsp dried marjoram)

Sugar

Salt

1 egg (medium-sized)

2 tbsp cream

250 g (1 cup) sour cream or heavy
   sour cream

These airy pastry pockets filled with Hungarian sauerkraut and mince seasoned with paprika are served with sour cream or heavy sour cream for the day's last rays.

———

Separate the puff pastry sheets for defrosting. Squeeze excess liquid from the sauerkraut, reserving the juice. Peel the onion and garlic. Mince the garlic and finely dice the onion. Heat the ghee in a frying pan. Add the mince, sauerkraut, onions, garlic and caraway and fry until the mince turns crumbly and the sauerkraut starts to take on colour. Dust with the two types of paprika powder. Coarsely chop the marjoram and stir into the mixture. Season with a pinch of sugar and salt. Add the sauerkraut juice and simmer, uncovered, until almost all of the liquid has evaporated. Transfer the mixture to a plate for cooling.

Preheat the oven to 180°C (350°F) (fan-forced; alternatively 200°C (390°F) conventional). Whisk the egg with the cream. Quarter the puff pastry sheets. Divide the filling among the sheets and brush the edges thinly with the egg and cream mixture. Fold the pastry over the filling and press the edges together to seal. Use a fork to create a serrated edge. Transfer the pastry pockets onto a baking tray, brush with the remaining egg and cream mixture and bake in the preheated oven, middle rack, until golden brown, about 15–18 minutes. Serve with lightly salted sour cream or heavy sour cream.

— EGÉSZSÉGEDRE! —

These pockets are delicious with a fresh, well-chilled cider.

NON-ALCOHOLIC: mix clear apple juice with the same volume of ginger ale.

ITALY

Italy – a place of yearning for so many –
is synonymous with great food. But there is in fact
no such thing as Italian cuisine.

Italy comprises 20 regions, which are divided into provinces. Over time, each of these regions, and even individual cities and towns, developed their idiosyncratic cuisines in line with historical, climatic and geographic conditions. The cultural history of Italian cooking therefore evolved gradually over centuries, giving rise to a virtually limitless number of recipes.

Pizza, for example. You may think it's a straightforward thing – not so! There are at least as many pizza dough philosophies in Italy as there are regions. The Neapolitans like a thin, soft crust. Only a few kilometres away, in Salerno, people insist on a much crisper crust. Quite often, crust texture is the subject of intense disagreement even within a town. And we are talking about something that is commonly regarded as one of the most straightforward of Italian dishes. Let's not even go into pasta here… But maybe we need to. The legendary Italian pasta chef Giuseppe di Martino once explained to me during a visit to Gragnano, the cradle of Italian pasta culture, that making pasta is an art: "We have been in the pasta secca business for about 2000 years," he said, with written records dating back over 500 years. "And once you have done something for 500 years, you really know how to do it," he stated with visible pride during a tour of his pasta manufactory, Pastificio dei Campi.

The selection of the right pasta type for a particular sauce is an art in itself already, he says. "Just take spaghetti Bolognese. It's a German invention. No true Italian would dream of serving his ragù with spaghetti! You eat and eat, and what are you left with on your plate at the end? The ragù! It's pointless! You need a type of pasta that the ragù clings to." Signore di Martino's disdain slowly gives way to a wide, conciliatory grin. "In Italy, we have developed hundreds of pasta shapes, and every single one of these shapes has its purpose. Each pasta deserves to be used optimally in the kitchen."

Consequently, there's quite a bit of complexity even to "simple" Italian cooking, yet it is always characterised by lightness and joyfulness. It doesn't come as a surprise that the Italians are also extremely fond of a good aperitif. Essentially, the twilight hour is a compulsory event that is often enjoyed over a bitter lemonade, an Aperol Spritz (p. 82) or a chilled glass of prosecco. Late afternoon drinks are always served with at least a small snack; juicy olives perhaps, a freshly baked focaccia (p. 82), a popular Caprese salad or crunchy risotto balls (p. 85), which are called arancini in Catania and arancina in Palermo. Whatever. Just drink in Italy's wonderful evening sun.

LIGHTNESS AND JOIE DE VIVRE IN ITALY

SUNSET WITH A VIEW

"When the sun goes down, and the shadows fall... something in my heart seems to say come back again, come back to old Capri", was a popular song even way back in the 40s. Amazing sunsets can be found not only on Capri, though – anywhere along the steep Amalfi coast is stunningly beautiful.

FOCACCIA & APEROL SPRITZ

Sunset at the Palazzo della Ragione in Padua. People gather to catch the evening light in the bars and cafés nestled underneath the old archways. Their tables are crowded with rounded glasses filled with ice cubes and a reddish orange liquid – the city's most famous beverage, the delectable Aperol Spritz. This is the city where it was invented. The waiter brings two wide glasses of them. They're ice-cold, frosted and hold two fat slices of peeled orange each. The aroma they give off is irresistibly fresh, partly due to the bitter Aperol liqueur, a distillate of rhubarb extract, bitter orange, cinchona bark, gentian and various secret herbs that gives this drink its inimitable flavour and oomph.

The brothers Luigi and Silvio Barbieri, natives of Venice, developed Aperol in 1919 and introduced the world to their new drink at the Padua International Fair in the same year. Their name, Fratelli Barbiere, still holds pride of place on the bottle label. We enjoy the drink, the gentle evening breeze, the Italian voices around us so much that I don't even hear the waiter arrive. He clears his throat and points to my glass with a stern expression on his face. "Yes, sure, another one, please," I say. He keeps looking at me sternly and points to the leftover slices of orange in my glass. Aaah! I understand. I pick a slice out of my glass and bite into it. It's the sweetest, fruitiest, juiciest orange I've ever had. The waiter acknowledges my instant bliss with a brief nod. When the security guy at the Aeroporto di Venezia-Tessera "Marco Polo" removes four oranges from my hand luggage the next day, I answer truthfully and with a shrug, "The other ingredients I can get at home."

———

FOCACCIA

For the starter, combine **190 g (¾ cup) plain flour (type 550)**, **190 ml (¾ cup) lukewarm water** and **1 g fresh yeast** the night before. Cover with a clean dish towel and leave to mature at room temperature for 12–15 hours.

Next day, combine the starter with **360 g (1½ cups) plain flour (type 550)**, **240 ml (1 cup) water**, **4 g fresh yeast** and **10 g salt** in the bowl of a food processor and process with a dough hook for 10 minutes. Transfer the dough to an oiled bowl, cover and leave to rise for 2.5 hours, removing the dough to stretch and fold it every 30 minutes.

Transfer the dough onto a baking tray brushed with **olive oil** and stretch out to form a flat bread. Leave to rise for 10 minutes. Use your fingers to press holes into the top and stretch the dough again a little. Set aside to rest for 10 minutes. Halve **8 cherry tomatoes**, sprinkle with a little salt and press into the dough, cut side up. Pick the leaves off **1 sprig each rosemary** and **thyme** and chop finely. Stir into **4 tbsp olive oil** and brush the dough with the mixture. Leave to rest for another 10 minutes. Preheat the oven to 250°C (480°F) and bake the focaccia on the middle rack until golden, about 25 minutes.

— CIN CIN! —

How to make a classic Aperol Spritz: pour **40 ml Aperol** over **ice cubes** in a highball or wine glass. Add **1 slice of organic orange**, peeled, and **70 ml dry Italian white wine**. Fill the glass with **70 ml ice-cold soda water** or **sparkling mineral water**.

NON-ALCOHOLIC: chilled Sanbittèr or Gingerino with ice cubes and orange slices.

ARANCINI DI RISO

INGREDIENTS

(makes 12 rice balls)

1 onion

1 garlic clove

2 tbsp olive oil

1 tbsp butter

200 g (1 cup) risotto rice

1 pinch ground saffron

100 ml (⅓ cup) white wine

500 ml (2 cups) hot vegetable stock

120 g (1¼ cups) Parmesan

Salt

Freshly ground black pepper

100 g (⅔ cup) peas

80 g ham

2 eggs (medium-sized)

6 tbsp flour (type 405)

200 g (1¾ cups) breadcrumbs

Oil for deep-frying

Arancini (literally: "small oranges") are traditionally Sicilian deep-fried risotto balls with a savoury filling. They come in round and cone shapes, and their name varies too: around Catania, they are conical like the local volcano, Mt Etna, and are called arancino, whereas in the Palermo region they are round like oranges and are called arancina. They can be filled with anything you like (or have left over): meat ragù, peas and ham, cheese and mushrooms. Recently these savoury rice balls have become a popular street food all over the world.

Peel and finely dice the onions; peel and mince the garlic. Heat some olive oil and butter in a saucepan and cook both until translucent. Stir in the rice and saffron and deglaze with white wine. Add a little of the hot stock. Continue to cook over medium heat, stirring constantly, until the liquid has almost evaporated, then add another ladleful of stock. Repeat until the risotto is cooked (about 20–25 minutes). Finely grate 80 g (¾ cup) Parmesan and stir into the cooked risotto. Season with salt and pepper. Set aside to cool, then refrigerate for several hours. Alternatively, cook the risotto the day before.

Boil the peas in salted water for 3 minutes. Refresh under cold water and drain. Dice the ham. Combine the ham and peas with 40 g grated Parmesan. Shape 1–2 tbsp risotto to a patty in your hand. Place a little of the filling into the centre and seal the risotto around it. Form into balls and set aside. Continue to shape about 12 balls.

Lightly beat the eggs. Turn the rice balls first in flour, then in the whisked egg. Roll in the breadcrumbs and press the breading in. Heat oil for deep-frying in a deep fryer according to the manufacturer's instructions. Alternatively heat the oil in a tall saucepan to 160–170°C (320–340°F).* Deep-fry the rice balls in the hot oil in batches until golden brown, about 2–3 minutes per batch. Drain on kitchen paper.

* If you do not have a cooking thermometer, test with a wooden spoon: Dip the spoon handle into the hot oil. The temperature is right if small bubbles start to rise.

MUSIC: *The fabulous Sicilian band of Roy Paci & Aretuska play upbeat ska jazz, reggae and Latin music. Guaranteed to get you into a good mood. Every single one of their albums is bellissimo, but I particularly like "Parola d'onore" (2004).*

CHICKPEAS WITH SPICED CHOCOLATE AND ORANGES

INGREDIENTS

(serves 4)

4 oranges

Orange liqueur (optional)

150 g semi-sweet cooking chocolate

2 fresh bay leaves

1 star anise

1 pinch cinnamon

2 tsp good cocoa powder

20 g sugar

100 ml cream

50 ml (¼ cup) milk

1 tin chickpeas (approx. 425 g net weight)

Signora Giovanna Voria of Agriturismo Corbella in the Cilento e Vallo di Diano National Park served me this unusual combination of chickpeas with bay leaf and dark chocolate when I visited there. Language difficulties prevented me from obtaining the precise recipe, but this reflects my culinary recollection of the dish.

———

Peel the oranges carefully, removing all of the white pith. Slice the oranges across and drizzle with a touch of orange liqueur (optional). Coarsely chop the cooking chocolate and transfer to a small saucepan. Add the bay leaves, star anise, cinnamon, cocoa powder, sugar, cream and milk and gently heat until the chocolate has melted. Drain the chickpeas and stir into the hot chocolate. Serve with the orange slices.

SERVE WITH: Vanilla ice cream. Oh yes.

MUSIC: *Matteo Brancaleoni recorded Italy's most beautiful and heartfelt pop songs on his 2015 album "Made in Italy" with a great deal of respect, and accompanied by a brilliant swing orchestra. Vo-lare!*

CIN CIN!

A shot of orange liqueur, pure and at room temperature, or with mint on ice.

BASTONCINI, CAPRESE SALAD & PEACHES WITH PARMA HAM

An Italian night, a feast of flavours and aromas, a homage to simple pleasures.

BASTONCINI DI POLENTA FRITTI WITH LEMON AND CAPER MAYONNAISE (serves 4–6)

For the mayonnaise: Combine **150 g (⅔ cup) mayonnaise** with **1 tbsp caper juice**, **1–2 tsp chopped capers**, **1 pinch finely grated organic lemon zest** and **1 tsp lemon juice**. Season with **salt**.

For the bastoncini: Purée **50 g (¼ cup) sundried tomatoes** with **1 garlic clove** in a blender. Transfer to a saucepan, add **1 litre (4 cups) vegetable stock** and bring to a boil. Gradually stir in **300 g (1⅔ cup) polenta** and simmer over low heat for 5 minutes. Stir in **50 g (½ cup) grated Parmesan**. Leave to cool slightly, then quickly whisk in **2 medium-sized eggs**, one at a time. Season with **salt**. Spread the polenta two finger widths thick on a tray lined with baking paper and leave to cool fully. Slice into fish finger-sized pieces. Heat a large non-stick pan and fry in batches until golden brown, using **2–3 tbsp olive oil** per batch. Drain on kitchen paper and serve with the mayonnaise and a **few caperberries**.

PEACHES WITH OLIVE OIL AND PARMA HAM (serves 4–6)

Cut **2–3 peaches** into wedges. Season with a little **sea salt** and freshly ground **black pepper** and drizzle with your best **olive oil**. Serve with **Parma ham**.

CAPRESE SALAD (serves 4–6)

Slice **4–6 oxheart tomatoes**. Season with **salt** and freshly ground **black pepper** and drizzle with your best **olive oil**. Arrange **4–6 small pieces of burrata** or **mozzarella di bufala** on top, salt again and drizzle with olive oil. Garnish with freshly picked **basil leaves**. Not part of the classic recipe, but good: drizzle with a little **balsamic vinegar**.

MUSIC:
An easy choice – any best-of album by Paolo Conte!

CIN CIN!

Open your favourite vino or prosecco or enjoy with an Aperol Spritz (p. 82).

1 Bastoncini di polenta
2 Peaches with Parma ham
3 Caprese salad

AUSTRIA

I've been to Austria many times. When I was still only
a boy, my parents often took me to the Austrian mountains,
to Vorarlberg and Bregenz, where I learned how to ski and
had my first taste of herb lemonade.

I have fond memories of summer holidays, too, of outdoor pools and me scooping orange ice cream from plastic oranges. The landlady at our holiday flat served an incredibly rich whipped cream with our afternoon coffee and cake. While we used our noisy electric mixer at home to produce something you could have easily sliced, our landlady whipped cream by hand, rhythmically, almost lovingly, and turned it into a delicate, light yet thickly viscous extravaganza that smoothly spread across our pieces of cake. That was my first ever lesson in culinary mindfulness and refinement.

It would be pointless to try to list all the Austrian delicacies that I've come to love. I'm very fond of a classic Vienna schnitzel, and on my last day on earth I'd love to have boiled beef; perhaps a top blade in a fragrant broth with warm marrow on toast, a side of chives sauce and creamed spinach, or green beans with dill and apple horseradish cream and a double serve of potato roesti – and then I might be ready to go.

However, I do hope that I'll still have plenty of time, and I'm therefore quite happy to make do with a cheese kransky from the Vienna Naschmarkt market or a hot, spicy Debrecen sausage with freshly prepared horseradish from any local food stall. Note that the Austrian word for horseradish is "kren", which comes from a Slavic word meaning "to cry".

I learned to appreciate yet another sausage specialty, the divine *bosna* (p. 103), in Salzburg. Trust me, it's worth a visit for this alone. And then I'm incredibly lucky to have found a publisher in Vienna! Ever since, I've visited the city quite often, and I always make sure I get to have a pot of Karlsbad coffee in the Sperl coffee house. Even at dusk. During my last visit, the resident pianist in the coffee house played Smetana's "The Moldau" – a touchingly beautiful moment.

I've also had the opportunity to explore the vineyards around Vienna, to enjoy the Heuriger new wine in Grinzing (p. 101) and to savour the menu of the busy "Zum Schwarzen Kameel" restaurant with my publisher's team for a few glasses of wine at sunset, served with delectable bread spreads, verhackerts (bacon spread) and saure blunzen (black pudding salad, p. 98). How utterly delightful. Oh, Vienna, I'll definitely be back.

OH, VIENNA, I'LL DEFINITELY BE BACK.

─ SUNSET WITH A VIEW ─

The left bank of the old and new Danube is highly recommended for evening sunseekers, as is the Gloriette in the park of Schönbrunn palace. The Belvedere Museum takes on a beautiful glow at sunset, or enjoy the last light on the Ferris wheel in the Vienna Prater.

THREE BREAD SPREADS

Slices of bread with a delicious spread are a fabulous Austrian invention that is somewhere between a sandwich and a canapé. The Art Nouveau bar of the Viennese restaurant "Zum Schwarzen Kameel" (Bognergasse 5) always stocks a wide selection of creative, high-quality sandwiches, lovingly presented in a long glass cabinet and served by the wonderful Erna Lenhardt. I suggest you come with a few of your favourite people and taste all of them. May the three varieties shown here give you a first, enticing impression.

SALMON

Combine a little **softened butter** with freshly chopped **chives**. Spread **slices of white bread or toast** thinly with the chives butter and top with slices of **smoked salmon or smoked Alaska pollock**. Trim off the crust and cut the bread into a neat rectangle. Garnish with **caperberries**.

BEETROOT (makes 4–6 slices)

Pulse **100 g beetroot (from a tin)**, **1 anchovy** and **1 tsp grated horseradish** in a blender to combine. Stir in **100 g (⅓ cup) cream cheese**, **1 tbsp mayonnaise** and **1 tbsp sour cream or heavy sour cream**. Season with **1 pinch curry powder** and **salt**. Trim the crusts off **4–6 slices rye bread**. Cut the slices into neat rectangles and spread with the cream. Sprinkle with **chopped chives** and serve.

HAM

This classic spread is also served on a roll at the Schwarzes Kameel, which makes its own hams. Trim the crust off **white bread or toast** and cut into rectangles. Spread thinly with **softened butter** and top generously with **high-quality ham (on the bone)**. Sprinkle with **grated horseradish** and serve.

— PROST! —

Enjoy with one or two glasses of Viennese Gemischter Satz DAC (Districtus Austriae Controllatus), a traditional wine made of at least three different varieties of grapes grown, harvested and processed in the same vineyard. These wines are very Viennese: the city has over 600 hectares of vineyards in its green belt.

MUSIC: *Viennese singer Valérie Sajdik published "Les Nuits Blanches", a breezy, cheerful album of chansons, in 2013. Other great choices for sundown are the excellent lounge albums by Saint Privat, a joint band project by the Viennese musician and producer Waldeck and Valérie Sajdik. The "Riviera" album (2004) has a great, relaxed groove.*

HEURIGER PLATTER

Take tram No. 38 out of the city towards the Viennese vineyards, all the way to the final stop in Grinzing, the centre of Viennese Heuriger culture, as my esteemed colleague Katharina Seiser said when she kindly took me there during one of my visits to Vienna. She highly recommended the "Buschenschank in Residence" by the winemaker team of Jutta Kalchbrenner and husband Marco of the Jutta Ambrositsch Vineyard (Himmelstrasse 7).

This vineyard offers the best Heuriger experience you could imagine. Several times a year, Viennese winemakers are permitted to serve and sell their wines directly, without a licence, for a strictly limited period to make room in their cellars for the next harvest. They serve little snacks on the side such as bread with black pudding, bacon spread, meat loaf, Liptauer cheese, savoury spreads and freshly prepared hot horseradish. Once you've been there, you'll always want to go back. Do make sure you check opening hours beforehand.

VERHACKERTS (BACON SPREAD) (serves 4–6)

Dice 250 g streaky, smoked bacon and mince finely in a food processor or meat grinder together with **5 sprigs marjoram** and **1 tsp caraway seeds**. Stir in **80 g rendered fat with crackling**, sprinkle with **2–3 tbsp chopped chives** and **serve on rye bread**.

SAURE BLUNZEN (BLACK PUDDING SALAD) (serves 4–6)

Whisk together **4 tbsp white wine vinegar**, **2 tbsp white wine**, **1 tbsp apple juice**, **1 tsp hot mustard**, **4 tbsp canola oil** and **4 tbsp olive oil** to make a vinaigrette. Season with **1 pinch sugar**, **salt** and **freshly ground black pepper**. Slice **450 g firm black pudding**. Peel **1 red onion** and slice into thin wedges. Cut **1 spring onion** into rings. Pick the leaves off **1 sprig marjoram**. Stir everything into the vinaigrette. Serve with **rye bread**.

SERVE WITH: Good cheese, speck, smoked pork sausages and horseradish.

MUSIC: *Kruder & Dorfmeister are among the best-known Austrian musicians internationally. This DJ and producer duo published their album "The K&D Sessions", a milestone in downtempo and lounge music, in 1998, and it still sounds as fresh as ever. Worth listening to again!*

PROST!

Gemischter Satz, Grüner Veltliner, any favourite wine.

BOSNA

The Balkan Grill in the heart of Salzburg (Getreidegasse 33a) is a tiny little window shop located in a narrow thoroughfare between Getreidegasse and the Pferdeschwemme ("Horse Pond"), which has become rather famous. This is where bosna originated, a modern classic of Austrian cooking consisting of a delicious grilled pork bratwurst (nadanitza) first imported from Bulgaria by Zanko Todoroff and originally served with white bread, onions and a curry spice mixture. He named his invention "bosa", the Bulgarian word for a snack, when he opened his tiny shop in 1950. However, the sign painter asked to make the shop sign misheard the word as "bosna", believing it to be connected to Bosnia and the Balkans, and Todoroff quite liked his mistake. Today, the Balkan Grill is owned by the Walters, a family of butchers, and Hildegard Ebener has sold this cult snack from the same shop window for over thirty years. Go visit for their range of bosna! But do try this DIY version of the sensational Salzburg hot dog to work up an appetite:

HERE'S HOW (makes 4 bosna)

Peel 4 small onions and cut into thin wedges. Season with **salt**. Heat **4 tbsp oil** in a pan over medium heat. Add the onion and sauté for 10–12 minutes. Meanwhile, heat a little oil in another pan and fry **8 of your favourite slender bratwursts**. Dust the cooked onions with **1 tsp mild curry powder** and **chilli** to taste. Remove from the heat and stir in **1 tsp mustard**. Chop **1 sprig curly parsley** and stir into the onion mixture. Peel and finely dice **½ red onion**. Season with **1 dash red wine vinegar** and salt. Halve **4 mini baguettes** or **white crusty rolls** and briefly toast under a hot oven grill, cut side up. Fill with the sausages and curried onions, top with the diced red onion and serve.

MUSIC: *Break beats, drum 'n' bass, electric sounds, heavy dub and sophisticated sound walls - the Viennese band Sofa Surfers does it all to perfection. Let their album "Transit" (1997) take you straight from the last light into the night.*

GERMANY

Germany. That's sausages and sauerkraut,
precision and cleanliness, punctuality
and cuckoo clocks.

The list of stereotypes about Germans is much longer, of course, and some of them are even believed by Germans themselves. For example that German food is mainly stodgy and more about feeding people than culinary pleasure. But once you look beyond the cliché of sausages and cabbage, you'll find a huge variety of delicious foods. Just think of all the amazing breads, beers and wines, potatoes and asparagus, oysters, crabs and plaice Germany has to offer.

I have my mother and grandmothers to thank for my love of German food. All three enjoyed cooking good food; my mother in the south, Oma Ruth all the way in the north, Oma Charlotte in the west of the country – and all of their kitchens had a bar stool that I'd climb on to be able to watch and help out. They took me on a childhood culinary road trip around Germany, with *maultaschen* (the German take on ravioli), *käsespätzle* (tiny dumplings with cheese and fried onion), pickled herring, *rote grütze* (red fruit jelly), sausages (of course!) and green herb sauce.

Food is always a big part of cultural identity, and a country's classic dishes also tell a story about its people. Germany's culinary map ranges from Frankonian pork roast to Leipizig mixed vegetables, Swabian beef stew, Thuringian dumplings, "heaven & earth" (mashed potatoes with apples) from the Rhineland, rollmops herrings from the north, Bavarian veal sausages with sweet mustard, Berlin-style fried liver, Hamburg fried fish in mustard sauce... true comfort food that warms your heart. However, the German soul seems to be less amenable to the cocktail hour as, at least traditionally, people used to work right through to dinner time. On their days off, however, they flock to beer gardens, wine bars or, later in the evening, to bars and pubs. And this is where we find their favourite snacks such as pickled eggs (p. 113), marinated cheese, *obatzda* cheese spread (p. 108) and rollmops (p. 110).

These are all culinary treasures, although a lot of knowledge of local crafts, products and recipes of German regional cooking is being lost, as more and more small farms, bakeries, local butchers' shops and pubs close down and their traditions vanish with them. Luckily, however, there has been a recent re-emergence of farmers, butchers, bakers, fishermen and cooks who strongly favour local variety. Farmers have started growing heritage produce instead of standardised varieties, they cultivate new varieties of crops and have returned to old breeds of livestock. There is lots going on there, with plenty of success, but this movement will need the interest and support of the wider public if the German culinary canon is to be expanded again. The world has become smaller, and this is why it's time to rediscover regional cooking, which is full of surprises, stories, history and, not least, flavours!

SOUL FOOD
THAT DELIGHTS:
GERMANY

— SUNSET WITH A VIEW —

A brief glance through sunset photos from
Germany in social media clearly shows that
the best pictures are taken somewhere
near water, whether that's the North
Sea, the Baltic, the Friesian islands, Lake
Constance or the Chiemsee, or the Rhine
or Main, Elbe, Danube, Neckar, Havel, Ems,
Saale or Spree rivers.

OBATZDA (CHEESE SPREAD)

INGREDIENTS

(serves 4–6)

200 g Camembert

200 g Limburger cheese

200 g paprika cream cheese

20 g (1½ tbsps) butter, softened

1 tsp caraway seeds

1 tsp sweet paprika powder

1–2 pinches hot paprika powder

Salt

80 g grilled capsicum, from a jar

1 small red onion

A few chives

Freshly ground black pepper

The golden hour is much loved in Bavaria, where people come together in beer gardens (or they have possibly sat there since lunchtime) and share some food as a foundation for the next beer. This savoury, very tasty obatzda cheese spread is up to the job!

———

All ingredients for obatzda should be at room temperature. Finely mash and combine the cheeses, cream cheese and butter with a fork, traditionally on a wooden board. Coarsely grind the caraway seeds and stir into the cheese mixture together with the paprika powders. Season lightly with salt and refrigerate until serving.

Drain the grilled capsicum and dice finely. Peel the red onion and slice into fine rings. Cut the chives into small pieces and garnish the obatzda with the capsicum, onion and chives. Serve sprinkled with freshly ground black pepper.

SERVE WITH: Sourdough bread, pretzels or pretzel rolls, red radishes, sliced cucumber and salted, thinly sliced white radish.

MUSIC: *The best brass music is clearly made in Munich, for example by Paco Mendoza and Don Caramelo, aka Raggabund, who play smooth reggae with a pinch of Latin and hip-hop. Recommended listening: their 2015 album "Buena Medicina".*

— PROST! —

Enjoy with a good lager, wheat beer or dark lager.

NON-ALCOHOLIC: pear juice with sparkling mineral water and a dash of cider vinegar.

ROLLMOPS

INGREDIENTS

(for 8 herring fillets)

1 carrot

3 small onions

½ tsp fennel seeds

1–2 tsp mustard seeds

2 bay leaves

6 juniper berries, lightly crushed

100 ml (½ cup) white wine vinegar

2 pinches salt

2 tbsp sugar

8 fresh herring fillets

Gherkins and toothpicks (optional)

Rollmops is so much more than hangover food! Served around sundown, it makes an excellent appetiser and pick-me-up food after a long day at work. Home-made, it is also a true delicacy with a subtly acidic flavour.

———

Peel and finely dice the carrot. Peel the onion and cut into thin wedges. Add the vegetables to a saucepan together with the fennel seed, mustard seeds, bay leaves, juniper berries, vinegar, salt, sugar and 400 ml (1½ cups) water. Bring to a boil and simmer, uncovered, for 8 minutes.

Meanwhile, rinse the herring fillets in cold water. Pat dry and transfer to a shallow baking dish, skin side up. Take the pickling liquid off the heat, leave to cool for 5 minutes and pour over the fish fillets. Leave to cool fully, cover and marinate in the refrigerator for 3–4 days.

At first it may seem like the fillets are about to fall apart, but resting them in the marinade restores their firm consistency so they can be served in the traditional way: wrapped around small gherkins and held together with toothpicks. Refrigerated, the pickled herrings will keep for 8–10 days in the liquid.

MUSIC: *The album "Nacht und Tag" ("Night and Day", 2017) by Berlin band 2raumwohnung makes for a perfect electro soundtrack for sunset. The "Day" side is quite chilled, while the "Night" side delivers sophisticated, pleasantly pulsing basses.*

— PROST! —

This goes well with a nice lager, pilsener or altbier.

NON-ALCOHOLIC: try with ginger ale with a crushed sprig of tarragon and a few thin slices of fresh cucumber, served on ice.

PICKLED EGGS

INGREDIENTS

(makes 12 pickled eggs)

12 eggs (medium-sized)

80 g sugar

50 g salt

150 ml (⅔ cup) vinegar

2 bay leaves

1 tbsp mustard seeds

1 tsp caraway seeds

2 onions, finely sliced

4 sprigs tarragon

Mustard

So-called "hunger stacks" were found in every Berlin pub worth its salt, all the way through from the golden 20s to the 70s. These were timber and glass cabinets on the pub counters, stacked with delicacies designed to keep the drinking public happily fed inside. Guests simply pointed to the snack of choice such as basic bread and dripping, cold rissoles, rollmops, sausages or eggs pickled in vinegar and salt, served with mustard.

———

Prick the eggs and boil them in salted water with a dash of vinegar for 10–12 minutes. Drain and cool in cold water. Bring 1 litre of water to a boil with the sugar, salt, vinegar, bay leaves, mustard and caraway seeds. Add the onions to the liquid and simmer for 5 minutes.

Peel the eggs and transfer them to clean screw-top or pickling jars together with the tarragon. Pour over the hot pickling liquid, seal the jars and leave to cool. Serve with mustard. Refrigerated, the eggs will easily keep for a week in the pickling liquid, and their flavour will develop from day to day.

MUSIC: *Ulrich Tukur and his Rhythmus Boys bring the "good old days" back to life in a very sophisticated way. Listen to their ode to the blue hour ("Eine blaue Stunde") that occurs around sunset on the album "Wunderbar, dabei zu sein" (2001, re-released in 2015).*

> A blue hour on a grey day
> That's the hour I yearn for.
> Because this short blue hour
> Is so rare
> Where you are so happy
> Where you are in a distant world.

— PROST! —

This goes well with a nice lager, pilsener or altbier.

NON-ALCOHOLIC: serve with an **Apple Shrub**: finely grate **4 apples**, combine with **150 g (½ cup) sugar** and **180 ml (¾ cup) cider vinegar**, cover and leave to marinate in the refrigerator for 2 days. Strain through a fine sieve, add a **dash of lemon juice** and top with ice-cold **sparkling mineral water**.

SWITZERLAND

It's high time to (re)discover one of the best traditional dishes of cheese-based Alpine cooking: simple, pared-down and entirely dedicated to the flavour of the main act – Raclette cheese.

RACLETTE

Rediscovering a true classic

INGREDIENTS

**200–250 g Raclette cheese
    per person (sliced about
    0.5 cm thick)**

300–350 waxy potatoes per person

1–2 tsp caraway seeds

1–2 tsp salt for the potatoes

**Freshly ground black pepper
    for the cheese**

1–2 jars mixed pickles or gherkins

Raclette is a Swiss institution that has been mangled beyond recognition as part of "all you can eat" home dinners that have elements such as prawns or even slices of salami under any type of melted cheese. (This is where native Swiss start to feel faint.) Modern raclette grills even feature integrated frying pans for things such as mini steaks, which are then served with heavy mayonnaise-based sauces, transforming a social dining experience into haphazard gluttony.

It's well worthwhile asking for and exploring different types of Raclette cheese, if you can. For a traditional Valais raclette, half wheels of cheese weighing a good three kilos each are placed inside a holder and grilled, sometimes over an open fire.* As the topmost layer melts, it is scraped directly onto diners' plates with a wooden scraper (the French word "*racler*" means "to scrape"), most commonly over potatoes boiled in water flavoured with a little caraway. This is served with pickled vegetables – that's all! Prepared in this way, raclette is just as easy to make at home. It does take a while and requires patience, but in good company it's great fun!

* Alternatively, you can use a purpose-made raclette grill, and follow the manufacturer's instructions in order to grill the cheese, potato, and then serve with the pickles as above.

PRÖSCHTLI!

Raclette is traditionally served with hot tea to aid with digesting the heavy cheese. However, at sunset it's delicious with a glass of light white wine, perhaps a full-bodied, pale yellow Vin du Valais Fendant AOC, a dry, fruity wine with a tingle of acidity. Fendant is the Valais name for Chasselas grapes, the most commonly grown variety in Switzerland.

CHEESE CRACKERS AND PESTO STICKS

The Swiss can be sticklers for their rules: commendably, they wouldn't dream of starting an evening or evening event without an "apéro", a fixture in Swiss culture that combines pleasure, company, chatting and networking. Excellent Swiss wines – most of which are never exported – are served with nibbles and local cured meats such as Bündnerfleisch, air-cured ham or salsiz sausages with noble mould.

CHEESE CRACKERS (makes 10–12)

Preheat the oven to 220°C (390°F). Finely grate **80 g young Sbrinz cheese** (alternatively young Parmesan) and season with a touch of **piment d'Espelette**. Transfer the cheese to a tray lined with baking paper, 1 tbsp at a time, and press into small, flat rounds, leaving a few centimetres in between. Bake in the preheated oven, middle rack, for 3–4 minutes. Remove from the oven and leave to cool fully on the tray. Serve with Bündnerfleisch.

PESTO STICKS (makes about 20)

Defrost 250 g puff pastry. Blend **1 bunch basil**, **½ garlic clove**, **1 tbsp toasted pine nuts**, **25 g grated Sbrinz cheese** (alternatively Parmesan), **6–8 tbsp olive oil** and **1 pinch salt** to make a firm pesto. Whisk **1 egg yolk** with **2 tsp cream**. Transfer the puff pastry sheets onto baking paper, spread thinly with pesto and cut them into 1.5 cm wide strips. Turn the strips over and brush the other side with the egg wash. Lift both ends of the strips off the tray and twist. Transfer the sticks to a tray lined with fresh baking paper and bake them in the preheated oven for 12–15 minutes. Serve with mild, pickled peppers.

PRÖSCHTLI!

These nibbles go well with light Swiss whites (Chasselas, Fendant) or rosés. Highly recommended: dry, gently peppery Dôle red wine cuvées from Valais – a perfect match for *Bündnerfleisch*.

MUSIC: *The Swiss hip-hop collective Sens Unik from Lausanne attracted a dedicated fan following between 1987 and its dissolution in 2010. They produced relaxed, predominantly French hip-hop music and had their greatest hit, "Original", a collaboration with the German band Die fantastischen Vier, in 1997. Rediscovering their work is truly worthwhile!*

CUISINE

DENMARK

The Danes quite like their herring. They have
it in innumerable variations: pickled, smoked, fried,
marinated or as salt-cured *matjes* herring.

HERRING PLATTER

A herring platter with chives and crispy onions on rye bread with a fried egg on the side is the perfect way to bring in the evening.

MARINATED MATJES (serves 4)

Briefly rinse **2 matjes butterfly fillets** in cold water. Pat dry and halve the fillets. Peel **1 red onion**, dice finely and combine with **3 tbsp white wine vinegar, 1 tsp aquavit, 1 tsp honey** and **3 tbsp canola oil** to make a vinaigrette. Drizzle the vinaigrette over the fish fillets. Serve garnished with **grated horseradish to taste**.

HERRING WITH BEETROOT (serves 4)

Slice **4–6 whole beetroots** from a tin. Peel and slice **1 shallot**. Toss with **3 tbsp red wine vinegar, 1 tbsp honey, 2 tbsp canola oil** and **1 tbsp nut oil** and season lightly with **salt**. Serve garnished with a few leaves of **dill** together with 2–3 drained, unrolled Danish *rullemops* (**rollmops/pickled herring**, p. 110).

CRISPY ONION BREAD WITH FRIED EGG (serves 4)

Spread **8 slices dark, Danish rye bread** (alternatively pumpernickel) to taste with **seasoned dripping or goose fat**. Finely chop **1 bunch chives** and sprinkle over the bread. Top with **4–6 tbsp Danish crispy fried onions**. Heat a mixture of **3 tbsp oil** and **1 tbsp butter** in a large frying pan and fry **4–8 medium eggs** for about 4–6 minutes. Season with salt. Optionally use egg rings to get the eggs perfectly round.

— SKÅL! —

A light lager or pilsener.

NON-ALCOHOLIC: iced cucumber lemonade flavoured with a sprig of dill.

SAVOY CABBAGE CHIPS

Lightly seasoned savoy cabbage leaves oven-baked until crisp make an unusual snack for the golden hour.

HERE'S HOW

Preheat the oven to 100°C (fan-forced, 210°F). **Wash 250 g savoy cabbage leaves** in hot water. Remove the cores and pat the leaves dry with kitchen paper. Toss thoroughly with **3 tbsp oil** in a bowl and spread across 2 trays lined with baking paper. Bake in the preheated oven for about 45 minutes. Open the oven door briefly after about 10 minutes to allow steam to escape. Continue to bake the chips, turning them twice. Serve sprinkled with **salt**. These chips are best eaten fresh and cannot be stored or prepared much in advance, as they quickly lose their crunch.

MUSIC: *The 2012 album "Watches Fall Asleep" by Copenhagen indietronica band Altmodisch ("Old-fashioned") features sophisticated downtempo electro pop in a gentle, even melancholy mood. As you listen to their soft stream of dotted beats and featherlight loops, let yourself be uplifted by soaring trumpets and drawn in by gently-picked banjos and cellos. Delightful!*

SKÅL!

These chips are particularly good with beer, but also go well with wine, sparkling wine or cocktails. A great match: a **Bloody Mary**!

For 1 glass, stir 40 ml chilled vodka with **150 ml cold tomato juice**, and **1 dash each lemon juice** and **Worcestershire sauce** (alternatively soy sauce) for about 15 seconds. Season with **celery salt**, **freshly ground pepper** or **Tabasco** and pour into a chilled glass.

For a NON-ALCOHOLIC Virgin Mary, substitute **2 tbsp pickle juice** for the vodka.

LEVERPOSTEJ

Danish liver pâté

INGREDIENTS

(serves 4)

Danish liver pâté:

200 ml (1⅓ cups) milk

30 g (4 tbsp) flour

25 g (2 tbsp) butter, diced

Salt, black pepper, nutmeg

400 g liver

100 g streaky smoked bacon

1 sprig summer savoury

4 sprigs marjoram

2 eggs (medium-sized)

200 g bacon, sliced

3 bay leaves

Tartar sauce:

200 g green cabbage

2 shallots

3 tbsp canola oil

100 g pickled gherkins

150 g mayonnaise

20 g mustard

1 tsp turmeric

1 pinch mild curry powder

1 tsp white wine vinegar

Salt, sugar

Sourdough bread, to serve

SKÅL!

A light lager or pilsener.

NON-ALCOHOLIC: chilled vegetable juice seasoned with salt, a dash of lemon juice and a touch of Tabasco.

Liver pâté, a Danish favourite, is delicious at any time of the day, whether for breakfast, as a generous *smørrebrød* or, of course, at the cocktail hour. Just as long as it's served with the famous Danish tartar sauce!

———

For the liver pâté, add the milk, flour and butter to a small saucepan and heat slowly, whisking continuously. Bring to a brief boil. Season the resulting bechamel sauce with salt, pepper and a pinch of nutmeg. Transfer to a bowl and leave to cool a little.

Process first the liver, then the streaky bacon together with the summer savoury and marjoram in a food grinder or processor. Whisk the mass into the bechamel sauce. Stir in the eggs, one at a time. Season with a little salt and pepper.

Preheat the oven to 170°C (340°F). Line a loaf tin with the bacon slices, leaving the ends to overhang. Top with the liver mixture. Place the bay leaves on top and fold the overhanging bacon slices over.

Transfer the tin inside a casserole dish. Pour in 3 finger widths of hot water and bring to a boil. Cook in the preheated oven for 60 minutes.

Meanwhile, prepare the tartar sauce: Pulse the cabbage in a food processor until finely chopped. Peel and finely dice the shallots. Heat the canola oil in a frying pan, add the cabbage and shallots and cook until translucent, about 4 minutes. Leave to cool. Finely dice the gherkins and combine with the mayonnaise, mustard, turmeric, curry powder and white wine vinegar until smooth. Add the cabbage and season with salt and a pinch of sugar.

Leave the cooked liver pâté to cool fully in the tin, then invert and serve in slices together with the tartar sauce and a good sourdough bread.

SWEDEN

This classic Swedish dish tastes even better home-made
than in your favourite Swedish furniture store – promise!
Serve with oven-baked potatoes with butter and sea salt
instead of mashed potatoes.

KÖTTBULLAR

INGREDIENTS

(serves 4)

4 large, floury potatoes
 (about 300 g each)

Olive oil

Salt

50 g breadcrumbs

200 ml (1⅓ cups) milk

1 tsp cornflour (cornstarch)

1 onion

Ghee for frying

500 g beef or pork mince

50 g (3 tbsp) butter (plus extra
 for the potatoes)

20 g (2½ tbsp) flour

350 ml (1½ cups) vegetable stock

100 ml (½ cup) cream

White wine vinegar

1 tsp soy sauce

1 bunch chives

4 sprigs dill

Coarse sea salt

Cranberry jam or compote

Preheat the oven to 200°C (390°F). Wash the potatoes and dry well; do not peel. Rub thinly with olive oil and a little salt. Transfer to a tray lined with baking paper and bake in the preheated oven until done, about 50–60 minutes. Start preparing the meatballs about 30 minutes before the potatoes are cooked.

Stir the milk into the breadcrumbs and cornflour and set aside to thicken. Peel and finely dice the onion. Heat a frying pan over medium heat, add 1 tsp ghee and fry the onion until translucent. Leave to cool. Knead the mince with the breadcrumbs and onions to combine well. Season with salt. Moisten your hands to shape the mass into balls about 3 cm (1¼ inch) in size.

Heat 1 tbsp ghee in a tall frying pan and fry the meatballs until golden brown, about 6–8 minutes. Remove the meatballs from the pan, cover and keep warm. Add the butter to the pan and melt, stirring. Dust with the flour, whisk in the cold stock in a steady stream and bring to a boil. Stir in the cream and simmer for 1 minute, whisking continuously. Season with a dash of white wine vinegar, soy sauce and salt. Cut the chives into short pieces, finely chop the dill and stir both into the sauce.

Remove the potatoes from the oven. Cut them open and serve with sea salt and butter to taste as a side for the köttbullar and sauce. Traditionally, this dish is also served with cranberries.

SMÖRGÅSBORD SLICES

Smörgåsbord, the ever-popular Swedish tradition of a generous, multi-course buffet of various delicacies, comes here in a somewhat reduced form for the cocktail hour: three delectable sandwiches.

PRAWN COCKTAIL (makes about 6–8 slices)

Whisk **6 tbsp firm mayonnaise** with **½ tsp curry powder** and **1 tbsp pineapple juice** until smooth. Season with **1 dash lemon juice** and a pinch of **cayenne pepper**. Chop **250 g cooked prawns** and combine with the mayonnaise. Spread on your favourite type of bread and garnish with **50 g trout caviar** and a handful of **cress**.

MATJES & CRAYFISH SALAD
(makes about 6–8 slices)

Finely chop **½ bunch dill** and combine with **3 tbsp cider vinegar, 2 tbsp apple juice, 1 tbsp honey, 1 tsp hot mustard** and **6 tbsp canola oil** to make a vinaigrette. Season with **salt, pepper** and a touch of **ground allspice**. Rinse **2 matjes butterfly fillets** in cold water, pat dry and cut into strips. Slice **8 gherkins**. Peel and halve **1 onion** and slice finely. Quarter **1 apple**, deseed and slice finely. Combine with the **crayfish** and toss everything with the vinaigrette. Divide among slices of your favourite bread.

COLD ROAST WITH CAPSICUM & MUSTARD MAYONNAISE (makes about 6–8 slices)

Whisk **6 tbsp firm mayonnaise** with **1 tbsp wholegrain mustard** and **1 tsp hot mustard**. Season with **1 dash tarragon vinegar** (alternatively white wine vinegar), **1 pinch sugar** and **salt**. Drain **80 g grilled capsicum** from a jar and cut into wide strips. Spread slices of your favourite bread with the mustard mixture and top with **250–300 g sliced cold roast** and the capsicum strips. Garnish with some finely chopped **chives**.

MUSIC: *The musician, singer and composer Jay-Jay Johanson creates intricate, light electro songs and melancholy lounge pop. His debut album "Whiskey" (1996) is just one of this Swedish downbeat crooner's works that makes for perfect background music to the end of the day.*

SPAIN

"Would you have a table for one, if possible outside?"
This is a phrase I've memorised in Spanish, and I also keep
it on a piece of paper inside my wallet, just in case.

My German-speaking hosts have a parent evening at their kids' school, and so I'm on my own at sunset. "I'll go out for a few tapas!" My hosts look somewhat concerned as they show me how to get from their place to the Plaça de Catalunya on a map. "This area you know," they explain, pointing vaguely to an area off the world-famous La Rambla. "You'll find really nice bars and tapas restaurants here."

Eating out can be difficult for solo travellers in Barcelona, as the major tapas restaurants all have bouncers to ensure that no valuable table for two is hogged by single guests. I repeat the question I have memorised again and again, only to be sent on my way with a brief "No!". However, I am undaunted and start exploring the narrow laneways off La Rambla. It's only a matter of minutes before I'm entirely lost in the maze of romantic alleys and tall, narrow buildings that make up the old city centre. There's laundry drying in the evening breeze above the heads of innumerable tourists in the streets, and a few street lamps shed a yellowy-orange light. I stop in a couple of bars I pass for a quick, ice-cold cerveza served in a frosted glass, but soon there's no denying it any longer: I'm hungry. I finally notice a tiny bar on a square outside a church. It

has a tiny menu of a few tapas, and I decide I'll just sit down at one of the three small tables without even asking.

The owner welcomes me with a "sí!" and wipes his dark hair from his face with a dish towel. I try my luck with English, saying that I'd like to eat something. "Ah! From Germany?", asks the owner, and his brow furrows as he asks, "Bayern München?" "No, no!", I reply, waving my hands. "Hamburgo! FC St. Pauli!" My host is delighted. "And we love Barça!" He points to the wall-sized FC Barcelona flag behind the counter: "Barça and St. Pauli are friends, so we are friends! My name is José!" We shake hands, and the first sherry is on the house. José brings me the menu: "Sorry, no kitchen, not much, but good!" he says, and that's exactly what it is. The *jamón ibérico* melts in the mouth, the chilled *boquerones en vinaigre* – tiny anchovies in mild vinegar – are fresh and the olives crunchy. José brings *croquetas de jamón* (p. 141) and a glass of red without even asking, and I don't mind at all. He accepts my compliments on the house specialties with a modest nod: "No problem, it is simple, it is product-kitchen." And then he sits down himself, putting a bottle of sherry and two glasses on the table.

PULPO Á LA GALLEGA

INGREDIENTS

(serves 4)

2 onions

Olive oil

800 g squid (frozen and defrosted)

1 tbsp red wine vinegar

650 g waxy potatoes

Salt

Freshly ground black pepper

Juice of 1 lemon

1 tsp sweet paprika powder

1 pinch hot paprika powder

A few sprigs flat-leaf parsley and basil

Soft-boiled squid with potatoes is a Galician national dish and a very popular tapa. Even today, *pulpo á feira* ("festive squid") is a must at any major event. This squid dish is traditionally served with potatoes on wooden boards.

———————

Peel and slice the onions, then sauté until translucent in 8 tbsp olive oil. Add the squid and top with water until it is just covered. Add the red wine vinegar, bring to a boil, cover and simmer over low heat until soft, about 1.5–2 hours.

Remove the squid from its broth and set aside. Peel and slice the potatoes. Strain the liquid through a sieve, season with salt and bring to a boil again. Add the potato slices and cook until done but still firm to the bite, about 8–10 minutes.

Meanwhile, clean the squid and cut into small pieces. Drain the potatoes and briefly rinse under cold water. They're best if still a little warm. Serve the potatoes and squid on a wooden board. Season with salt and pepper, drizzle with lemon juice to taste and plenty of olive oil. Dust with the two types of paprika powder and garnish with freshly picked parsley and basil leaves.

* Using frozen squid is perfectly fine, as freezing makes it tender, and you won't need to pound it for tenderising – in the classic version, the freshly caught squid is pounded against the nearest harbour wall.

MUSIC: *Ojos de Brujo is a band that has unfortunately disbanded. Their distinctive mix of styles, ranging from Latin to hip-hop flamenco, funk and rumba, made them Spanish superstars. Their 2002 album "Bari" would be my first choice for a Spanish blue hour.*

ALCAFOCHAS CON ANCHOVAS

I gaze up into the dark blue sky above Jerez de la Frontera. The shadows are growing longer; the perfectly chilled sherry in my glass smells fabulous and melts in my mouth. It's a Manzanilla sherry from Sanlúcar de Barrameda, pale yellow with aromas of almonds, green herbs, salt and a tinge of wood. This is where sherry comes from: the "sherry triangle" between Sanlúcar de Barrameda, El Puerto de Santa María and Jerez de la Frontera in south-western Spain.

Over the past few days, I have visited countless bodegas and enjoyed Spanish hospitality everywhere. The large sherry producers offer guided tours, and they share their pride in the unique, complex wines they make in this region with the smaller bodegas. I'm sitting outside the tapas bar El Gallo Azul, and the waiter brings me small artichokes wrapped in anchovies and drizzled with basil oil. Very simple, very delicious and utterly delightful with the very dry Fino in the chilled glass in front of me.

HERE'S HOW (makes about 16)

DRAIN **2 jars of artichoke hearts (370 g net weight each)** and pat dry with kitchen paper. Rinse **16 anchovies** under cold water. Pat dry with kitchen paper and wrap around the artichokes. Secure with skewers or toothpicks. Purée **100 ml (1 cup) olive oil** with **1 bunch basil**, season lightly with **salt** and drizzle over the artichokes.

MUSIC: *The Spanish singer and composer Concha Buika ("Buika") combines flamenco and traditional copla andaluza with soul, jazz and funk elements. Her 2013 album "La noche más larga" is particularly beautiful.*

— SALUD! —

A dry Fino sherry, refreshing Manzanilla sherry, an Oloroso or Amontillado are all great. Be sure to serve the sherry chilled or even very cold, best in wine glasses so that its complex aromas can develop fully.

4

5

PA AMB TOMÀQUET & PIMIENTOS DE PADRÓN, AIOLI (AND SANGRÍA)

Three classic dishes of Catalan and Mallorcan tapas culture, plus the (in)famous sangría – here's hoping that this recipe will restore its formerly excellent reputation!

PA AMB TOMÀQUET (serves 4–6)

Drizzle 12 slices pan moreno (unsalted white bread) generously with **olive oil** and toast until light brown on both sides, either in a frying pan or under the oven grill. Peel and halve **2 garlic cloves** and rub the toasted bread with the cut sides. Quarter **3 very ripe tomatoes** and mash them onto the bread slices. Season with **fleur de sel** and serve drizzled with olive oil.

PIMIENTOS DE PADRÓN (serves 4–6)

Fry 300 g pimientos de padrón in 6 tbsp olive oil in a large non-stick pan for 3–5 minutes. Serve sprinkled with **sea salt**.

AIOLI (makes about 100 ml)

Purée 1 garlic clove with **50 ml (½ cup) milk** and **1 pinch salt** with a handheld blender. Combine **50–80 ml (3-5 tbsp) vegetable oil and olive oil** (mixed 1:1) and whisk into the mixture, first drop by drop, then in a thin stream. Refrigerate. This mayonnaise will keep for 1–2 days in the refrigerator but tastes best on the day it is made.

SALUD!

Just about any of your favourite Spanish wines goes well with tapas. However, it might be time to restore the reputation of **sangría**, which has sadly become synonymous with sweet plonk. This is how you prepare it correctly, with style:

Peel and dice **3 unwaxed oranges** and **1 lemon**, removing all of the white pith. Dice **3 peaches**. Combine the fruit with **1 tbsp sugar** and transfer to a carafe. Add 2 handfuls of ice cubes. Combine **50 ml red port wine** with **50 ml orange liqueur** and **3-4 dashes angostura bitters**. Pour the mixture over the fruit and add **1 litre light, chilled red wine**. Divide ice cubes among tumbler glasses and pour the sangría.

NON-ALCOHOLIC: combine the fruit for the sangría with an ice-cold mixture of **cherry juice**, **redcurrant juice** (mixed 1:1), **50 ml orange cordial** and **50 ml elderflower cordial** and top up with chilled sparkling mineral water.

CROQUETAS DE JAMÓN

INGREDIENTS

(serves 4–6)

1 onion

1 garlic clove

200 ml (¾ cup) beef stock

200 ml (¾ cup) milk

50 g (6 tbsp) flour

50 g (3 tbsp) butter, softened

50 g ham

50 g serrano ham

½ bunch flat-leaf parsley

1 tbsp mature manchego
  cheese, grated (alternatively
  Parmesan)

1 pinch nutmeg

½ tsp finely grated lemon zest
  (best organic)

Salt

Freshly ground black pepper

200 g (1¾ cups) breadcrumbs

3 eggs (medium-sized)

Oil for deep-frying

Ham croquettes are a classic Spanish tapa, prepared with the best, air-cured serrano ham. But I prefer this exquisite ham raw, in paper-thin slices. This is why I have replaced half of the serrano ham by plain ham in my version of these croquettes. This makes for croquettes that have a bit of bite from the softer ham as well as the rich flavour of serrano.

———

Peel and finely dice the onion. Peel and mince the garlic. Combine both with the stock, milk, flour and butter in a saucepan and heat, whisking quickly. Switch to stirring with a wooden spoon and bring the mixture to a boil. Continue to simmer the bechamel sauce for another 2–3 minutes, stirring continuously, then remove from the heat.

Finely dice the ham and serrano ham. Chop the parsley finely and stir both into the bechamel sauce together with the manchego cheese. Season with nutmeg, lemon zest, salt and pepper. Leave to cool, cover and refrigerate for 3–4 hours until set.

Lightly beat the eggs. Use moistened spoons to shape the refrigerated mixture into small croquettes. Turn these first in the breadcrumbs, then in the egg and again in the breadcrumbs. Press the breading in gently. Leave the croquettes to rest and dry a little for 15–20 minutes before deep-frying.

Heat oil in a deep fryer according to the manufacturer's instructions. Alternatively heat the oil in a tall saucepan to 190°C (370°F).* Deep-fry the croquettes in batches until golden brown, about 2–3 minutes per batch. Drain on kitchen paper.

* If you do not have a cooking thermometer, test with a wooden spoon: Dip the spoon handle into the hot oil. The temperature is right if small bubbles start to rise.

MUSIC: *Limbotheque, with their amazing singer Carol Garciá, are a Valencia band that combines classic jazz with tejano music, Balkan beats, surf, Charleston and Latin on their albums, all served with Mediterranean lightness.*

CHURROS MÁLAGA

INGREDIENTS

(serves 4)

Churros:

25 ml (1½ tbsp) Málaga wine

20 g (1½ tbsp) butter

1 pinch cinnamon

1 tsp organic lemon zest

125 g (¾ cup) flour (type 405), sieved

1 egg (medium-sized)

1 pinch baking powder

Oil for deep-frying

Icing sugar, for dusting

Chocolate sauce:

175 g semi-sweet cooking chocolate

30 g (¼ cup) sugar

2 tbsp cocoa powder

1–2 pinches cinnamon

Salt

—— SALUD! ——

Enjoy with coffee and/or a small glass of Málaga wine, served in a tumbler over 1–2 ice cubes and garnished with a strip of orange zest.

NON-ALCOHOLIC: dilute orange cordial with water to taste and also serve over ice and with orange zest.

The Cafetería Casa Aranda in the heart of Málaga has made a culinary trinity of scrumptious, hot churros, strong coffee and fragrant hot chocolate since 1932. There's a hole in the cafeteria wall that allows guests to watch veritable mountains of the hot pastries being made. For the original you'll have to go to Málaga, but my attempt is as close as I can get!

————

For the churros, bring the Málaga wine to a boil, then add 200 ml (¾ cup) water, the butter, cinnamon and lemon zest. Stir in the sieved flour and combine everything to a smooth dough, stirring continuously with a wooden spoon. Continue to stir for another 1–2 minutes. Transfer the dough to a mixing bowl and mix in the egg with an electric mixer. Leave the dough to cool, then knead in the baking powder.

For the chocolate sauce, break the cooking chocolate into pieces. Transfer to a saucepan together with 200 ml (¾ cup) water, the sugar, cocoa powder, cinnamon and a tiny pinch of salt. Gently heat to melt, stirring continuously, until you have a glossy sauce. Set aside.

Heat plenty of oil in a deep-fryer according to the manufacturer's instructions; alternatively use a deep saucepan and heat the oil to about 180°C (350°F).* Transfer the dough into a piping bag fitted with a fluted nozzle and pipe 10 cm (4 inch) lengths straight into the hot oil, using a sharp knife to cut it into lengths. Deep-fry the churros in batches until golden brown, about 6–8 minutes each. Serve hot with the chocolate dipping sauce, dusted with icing sugar to taste.

* If you do not have a cooking thermometer, test with a wooden spoon: Dip the spoon handle into the hot oil. The temperature is right if small bubbles start to rise quickly.

MUSIC: *Manu Chao's masterful 1998 album "Clandestino" is still great, every time. "Mama was queen of the Mambo, Papa was King of the Congo, Deep down in the jungle, I started bangin' my first bongo…"*

MOROCCO

Pastilla (or *b'stella*) is a festive dish that takes a bit of effort to make. It's usually served warm as an entrée.

FISH & PRAWN PASTILLA

INGREDIENTS

(serves 6)

250 ml (1 cup) fish stock

400 g white fish fillet, deboned
(e.g. cod)

300 g prawns

120 g (½ cup) butter, softened

1 packet ground saffron (0.1 g)

30 g flour

Salt

Cayenne pepper

2 onions

2 tbsp olive oil

2 eggs (medium-sized)

12 sheets filo or yufka pastry

150 g (1 cup) salted, smoked
almonds

Cinnamon

1 tsp sugar

1 tsp ras el hanout (Moroccan
spice mix)

Crisp pastilla pastries come with meat, fish or seafood fillings, but despite the savoury fillings, they always also include a sweet note. In Morocco, this dish is often dusted with cinnamon and icing sugar before serving.

Bring the fish stock to a boil, add the fish and simmer gently over low heat until cooked, about 5 minutes. Chop the prawns. Lift the fish from the stock with a slotted spoon and pull it apart with a fork. Knead 40 g (2½ tbsp) butter with the flour to combine. Whisk the saffron and butter and flour mixture into the hot stock and simmer for 2 minutes, whisking continuously. Season with salt and cayenne pepper, remove from the heat and set aside to cool a little.

Peel and halve the onions and slice finely. Season with salt and fry in the oil until golden, about 10–12 minutes. Leave to cool. Meanwhile, whisk the eggs until smooth, then stir in 3 tbsp of the saffron sauce. Return the mixture to the remaining saffron sauce. Heat the sauce to almost boiling and leave to cool again.

Melt the remaining butter and brush a round pie dish (about 30 cm ø) thinly with butter. Brush the pastry sheets thinly with butter. Line the pie dish with 8 overlapping pastry sheets, leaving the pastry to overhang. Place another pastry sheet in the middle of the dish. Set aside the remaining butter.

Preheat the oven to 200°C (390°F). Pulse the fried onions and almonds with a touch of cinnamon, sugar and ras el hanout in a food processor to combine. Spread the saffron cream, fish and prawns across the pie bottom. Cover with the almond and onion mixture. Fold the overhanging pastry sheets over the filling and top with the remaining 3 pastry sheets overlapping somewhat. Press the edges inside the pie dish. Brush the top with the remaining butter. Bake in the preheated oven until golden brown, about 20–25 minutes.

HUMMUS SANDWICH
WITH DUKKAH

I ate this amazing sandwich in The Breakfast Club in Amsterdam rather than in Casablanca: creamy hummus with pickled capsicums and onions on bread, sprinkled with crunchy, savoury dukkah, a North African mixture of nuts and spices that is absolutely addictive and goes with just about anything. Especially with these sandwiches!

HERE'S HOW (makes 6–8 sandwiches)

For the hummus:

Drain **1 tin chickpeas (425 g net weight)** and blend until creamy with **200 g tahini (sesame paste)**, **1–2 tbsp lemon juice**, **½ garlic clove** and 2–4 tbsp water. Season the hummus with **salt** and a touch of **piment d'Espelette** (alternatively cayenne pepper).

For the dukkah:

Finely grind **1 tbsp fennel seeds, 1 tbsp coriander (cilantro) seeds, ½ tsp cumin, 1 tsp black peppercorns, 1 tbsp toasted sesame seeds** and **1 tsp black sesame seeds** in a mortar and pestle. Add **80 g roasted, salted peanuts** and continue to grind until you have a fine spice mixture.

For serving:

Peel and halve **1 red onion**, slice finely and season with **1 tsp red wine vinegar** and **salt**. Drain the **pickled capsicum** (p. 74), wash and spin dry **1 handful of rocket**. Spread **6–8 slices of bread** with the hummus, top with the capsicum, pickled onions and rocket, sprinkle with dukkah and serve.

—— BSSAHA! ——

Place fresh mint leaves in a tea glass and pour over hot water. Sweeten to taste with honey or raw sugar.

MUSIC: *The singer Oum interweaves traditional sounds of Morocco with a generous side of jazz on her 2013 debut album " Soul of Morocco" – very sophisticated!*

BRIOUAT PASTRIES

with minced meat, spinach & pine nuts

INGREDIENTS

(makes 24 briouats)

1 tbsp raisins

100 ml (½ cup) grape juice

25 g (3 tbsp) pine nuts

1 onion

1 garlic clove

Sunflower oil

150 g minced beef

100 g minced lamb (alternatively more minced beef)

100 g baby spinach leaves

1–3 pinches ras el hanout (Moroccan spice mix)

Salt

1 tbsp honey

Chilli sauce

50 g (⅓ cup) feta

6 filo or yufka pastry sheets

1 egg

These crunchy pastry pockets, stuffed with a wide variety of fillings, are a popular Moroccan snack.

———

Boil the raisins and grape juice in a small saucepan until the liquid has all but evaporated. Dry-roast the pine nuts in a pan until golden brown. Peel the onion and garlic. Mince the garlic and finely dice the onion. Heat 2 tbsp oil in another large pan and sauté the onion and garlic until translucent. Add the mince and fry until crumbly. Add the spinach and stir in until wilted. Season the mixture with ras el hanout, salt, honey and chilli sauce. Add the raisins and pine nuts. Leave to cool, then crumble in the feta.

Preheat the oven to 200°C (390°F). Brush the pastry sheets thinly with oil and place them onto a cutting board, oiled side down. Cut each sheet into 4 evenly wide strips. Place 1 tbsp of the filling onto the bottom end of each strip. Fold the bottom edge of the pastry over the filling to make a neat triangle encasing the filling. Keep folding the triangle over and to the side until you have a well-sealed pastry parcel. Whisk the egg, brush the final edges with the egg wash and press to seal. Transfer the briouats to a tray lined with baking paper and bake in the preheated oven for 20–25 minutes.

MUSIC: *Rachid Taha, a singer and musician living in France, is a superstar of modern Maghreb music. His albums mix traditional North African musical styles such as chaâbi and raï with French chansons and rock influences. His 1998 album "Diwân" features more traditional sounds.*

BELGIUM

Liège waffles are a Belgian specialty. They are a little chewier and richer than other types of waffles, and they are traditionally made with pearl sugar, which makes the waffles caramelise lightly during baking.

LIÈGE WAFFLES

Gaufres de Liège

INGREDIENTS

(makes about 8 waffles)

For the waffles:

1 vanilla pod

20 g (1½ tbsp) sugar

150 ml (½ cup) milk

20 g yeast

150 g butter

2 eggs (medium-sized)

1 pinch salt

400 g (2⅔ cups) flour (type 405)

150 g pearl (nib) sugar

For the cherry compote and
  vanilla sour cream:

500 g sweet cherries

1 tbsp sugar

500 ml (2 cups) cherry juice

1 strip organic lemon zest

1 tsp cornflour (cornstarch)
  (about 5 g)

155 g (10 tbsp) vanilla yoghurt

2 tbsp sour cream or heavy sour
  cream

A dash lemon juice

The characteristic, somewhat uneven edges and typical pattern of Liège waffles are only produced by a classic Belgian waffle iron.

———

For the waffles, halve the vanilla pod lengthwise and scrape out the seeds. Transfer the pod and seeds to a small saucepan together with the sugar and milk. Warm gently and dissolve the yeast in the mixture. Melt the butter in another small saucepan. Lightly beat the eggs.

Remove the vanilla pod from the milk mixture. Place the flour in a mixing bowl and add the lukewarm milk and butter together with the eggs and salt. Combine everything to a dough with the dough hook of a food processor or hand mixer. Knead for 5 minutes. Cover and leave to rise in a warm place for 45 minutes.

Meanwhile, prepare the cherry compote: wash, pit and halve the cherries. Bring the cherry juice, sugar and lemon zest to a boil in a saucepan and simmer, uncovered, to reduce by half. Whisk the cornflour with 1 tbsp water. Remove the lemon zest, return the mixture to a boil and gradually stir in the cornflour. Simmer for 1 minute, whisking continuously. Add the cherries to the hot mixture and leave to cool.

For the vanilla sour cream, combine the vanilla yoghurt with sour cream or heavy sour cream and season with lemon juice.

Just before baking the waffles, knead the pearl sugar loosely into the dough. Preheat the waffle iron and bake the dough in 8 small portions until golden brown, about 3–4 minutes at medium heat.

— PROST! SANTÉ & PROOST! —

Belgian waffles go well with coffee,
sparkling wine or chilled kriek lambic,
a Belgian cherry beer.

MUSSELS IN BEER BROTH

Mussels are a true staple of Belgian cuisine, which has countless recipes for them: with wine and cream, with curried cream and, of course, with beer. After all, Belgium is a beer-loving nation, with its highly hopped lambic beers, a "dry" style of beer with low carbon content that is delightfully acidic and very refreshing. The finely acidic gueuze beers are also amazing. These are made from a lambic brew that is left to mature in the bottle, like champagne, and produces very fine bubbles in the glass. It also makes an excellent combination with mussels!

HERE'S HOW (serves 4)

Wash 1.5 kg mussels in cold water and trim off the beards. Discard any mussels that are already open and do not close under gentle pressure. Peel and finely dice **1 carrot**. Peel and finely dice **50 g celery**. Slice and wash **50 g leeks**. Slice **20 g ginger**, unpeeled. Peel and finely slice **1–2 garlic cloves**. Melt **50 g butter** in a large saucepan. Add the vegetables, **2 bay leaves**, **1 tsp mustard seeds** and **1 tsp sugar** and fry until translucent, stirring frequently. Pour in **200 ml lambic beer** (alternatively another type of acidic beer) and bring to a boil. Add the mussels and some salt, stir, cover and cook for 8 minutes.

SERVE WITH: French fries (p. 170) or bread.

PROST! SANTÉ & PROOST!

Drink with chilled lambic or gueuze beer.

NON-ALCOHOLIC: chilled verbena tea, mixed with cloudy apple juice and topped up with sparkling mineral water.

POPCORN THREE WAYS

Brussels is a very international city, and the cocktail hour in any pub can almost look and sound like a NATO member state meeting. But regardless where they're from, people love to go for a shared lambic beer after a hard day's work, perhaps with some salted popcorn on the side, perhaps with popcorn seasoned three ways, just so there's bound to be consensus.

BASIC POPCORN RECIPE (serves 4–6)

Heat **2 tbsp oil** in a large saucepan with a lid. Add **120 g popcorn kernels** and shake well. Sprinkle with **salt**, cover and place over medium heat. Shake the saucepan occasionally. The popcorn will start popping after about 7 minutes. After another 3 minutes or so, the popping will slow down. Remove from the heat. Melt **2 tbsp butter** and toss with the warm popcorn in a bowl. Best served immediately.

PAPRIKA & PIMENT D'ESPELETTE POPCORN

Add ½ **tbsp sweet paprika powder** and a little **piment d'Espelette** to taste to the melted butter.

AONORI POPCORN

Aonori, that is dried, finely chopped nori seaweed, is available from Asian supermarkets and some health food stores. For aonori popcorn, combine the melted butter with **1 tbsp aonori** and **chilli flakes to taste**.

CURRIED POPCORN

Add ½ **tbsp mild curry powder** and a little **piment d'Espelette** to taste to the melted butter.

MUSIC: *"Oyebo Soul", the Belgian band Arsenal's 2003 debut album, fuses world beats with electronica. There are African influences, Latin and lounge, polyphonic vocals, hip-hop beats and pulsating basses, yet Hendrik Willemyns and John Roan's music is always totally relaxed – ideal for a chilled start to the evening.*

FRANCE

Our French honeymoon in a rusty old station wagon
was twelve days long, meaning twenty-four meals.
Where better than in France…

We ate amazing hand-ground steak tartare at a roadhouse, had mussels at the beach of Saint-Jean-Cap-Ferrat and liver crème brulée at Chez Yvonne's in Strasbourg. In Aubrac, we ordered a juicy, aromatic steak of Aubrac beef with aligot de montagne, a traditional regional dish of cheesy mashed potatoes.

That was in a crowded bar in the town of Laguiole, which is internationally renowned for its knives. The TV in the bar showed the rugby World Cup finals, and when I asked the French lady sitting next to me to please pass the salt, she winked at me and produced a tin of fleur de sel salt she carried with her in her handbag. Merci, madame!

We then went to Bordeaux. The street signs in and around Bordeaux bring to mind some very good wines: St. Émilion, Pomerol, Entre-Deux-Mers… the region's country roads are lined with expansive vineyards. The region has well over 7,000 châteaux, and every turn-off seems to lead to yet another winery with yet another promising name. In Libourne, we caught the town's market day, where we marvelled at the mounds of fresh, colourful vegetables and aromatic ceps and tasted exquisite ham sliced straight off the bone with a long knife. The farmer explained solemnly that it came from a truly outstanding pig, his favourite

pig, in fact, with the best legs in the entire region, no kidding. He handed us some paper-thin slices with an expectant smile. We chewed with our eyes closed to savour the experience fully.

The next stand had a vat full of pure white, small prawns that smelled delicious. These delicate shellfish called crevettes blanches are fished at the mouth of the Gironde river and cooked straight away in salt water with bay leaves and star anise. We bought a bag and found out that the crevettes are a popular snack to have with an aperitif as the shadows lengthen. You simply remove the head and eat the tail, which has a nutty flavour, together with its crispy, paper-thin skin.

At the end of our trip, at the Côte d'Azur, we savoured the absolutely simple, produce-based cuisine of minimalist chef Laurent Poulet. How little it takes! The great Alain Ducasse once explained that cooking is easy: all you need is perfect produce, knowledge of how to prepare it correctly, and the perfect cooking time. Oh, France! We really should go back soon. For an aperitif, perhaps, or a few oysters (p. 161), for a salade Lyonnaise (p. 162) or a galette from Auvergne (p. 166)… let's just keep going…

FRANCE:
WHERE PLACE
NAMES MELT IN
THE MOUTH

Désignations	VOLUME SERVI	PRIX COMPTOIR	SALLE TERRASSE
CAFÉ noir	la tasse	2,20	2,20
BIÈRE pression	0,3 L	2,80	2,80
BIÈRE le flacon	0,3 cl	3,60	3,60
JUS de FRUITS	0,2 L	2,30	2,30
SODA	0,25	2,60	2,60
EAU minérale	0,75 L	6,00	6,00
EAU gazeuse	0,46 L	2,00	2,00
APÉRITIF anisé	2 cl	3,30	3,30
PLAT du JOUR			
SANDWICH	merg	7,90	7,90

1 Oyster vinaigrette
2 Cider oysters
3 Oysters en croûte d'herbes

OYSTERS THREE WAYS

French oysters are world-famous. Among the best are harvested in the bay of Arcachon, a seaside resort on the Atlantic coast, about 60 km south-west of Bordeaux. The town of Riec-sur-Bélon in Brittany is renowned for its delicious Bélon oysters. The fleshy Gillardeau oysters and supreme Fines de Claire rock oysters grow in Marennes, between the Charente coast and Île d'Oléron, the former in natural basins (called claires in French).

SHUCK AWAY!

Fresh oysters are a taste sensation, even au naturel. To crack them open, place them in a folded dish towel with the lid facing up. Use a shucking knife (or a screwdriver) to carefully lever the oyster open, starting from the tip. Protect your hand with a shucking glove. Sever the oyster muscle and pry the shell open. Separate the oyster meat from the shell. Remove any shell splinters from the oyster juice but keep the juice itself! Serve the oysters on ice straight from the shell. Make sure you chew the oyster so that it releases its full aroma.

TASTY OPTIONS:

OYSTER VINAIGRETTE (for 6–8 oysters)

Quarter, deseed and finely dice **1 tomato**. Peel and finely dice **1 shallot**. Combine with **1–2 tsp white wine vinegar, 2 tbsp dry white wine** and **1 tsp olive oil** and leave to marinate. Season with a touch of **salt** and **piment d'Espelette**.

CIDER OYSTERS (for 6–8 oysters)

Finely dice ½ **green apple**. Peel and finely dice **1 shallot**. Combine with **4 tbsp cider, 1–2 tsp cider vinegar** and **1 tsp olive oil** and leave to marinate. Season with a touch of **salt**.

OYSTERS EN CROÛTE D'HERBES (for 6–8 oysters)

Blend **1 sprig lemon thyme** and **4 sprigs flat-leaf parsley** with **40 g breadcrumbs** and **30 g olive oil**. Season lightly with **salt**. Spread the mixture on the oysters and place under a hot grill for a few seconds until the topping just starts to take on colour.

À VOTRE SANTÉ!

Champagne! Or a nice vintage sparkling wine. Among white wines, I recommend a Muscadet, Entre-Deux-Mers, Sancerre, Chablis or Sauvignon Blanc, best very well chilled.

SALADE LYONNAISE

INGREDIENTS

(makes 4 salads)

2 shallots

Olive oil

2 tbsp hearty chicken stock

White wine vinegar

1 tsp Dijon mustard

1 tsp wholegrain mustard

Sugar

Salt

½ garlic clove

100 g streaky bacon, sliced

180 g curly endive lettuce

2 slices white bread

2 sprigs lemon thyme

1 tbsp butter

4 eggs (medium-sized)

Freshly ground black pepper

The French version of a Caesar salad fuses sophisticated simplicity with complex aromas.

————

Peel and finely dice the shallots. Heat 6 tbsp olive oil in a frying pan, add the shallots and cook until soft, about 2–3 minutes. Remove from the heat, transfer to a bowl and leave to cool slightly, then whisk with the stock, 4 tbsp white wine vinegar, both types of mustard and a pinch each of sugar and salt to make a vinaigrette. Place the half garlic clove in the vinaigrette to marinate.

Preheat the oven to 200°C (390°F). Cut the bacon slices into three strips each; transfer to a tray lined with baking paper and bake until crisp, about 15 minutes. Break the lettuce into bite-sized pieces and wash in warm water. Spin dry.

Dice the bread into crouton-sized pieces. Chop the lemon thyme. Heat 1 tbsp each olive oil and butter in a pan until foamy. Add the croutons and toast over medium heat until golden brown. Add the thyme, season with salt, toss once more and drain on kitchen paper.

For the poached eggs, add water and 2 tbsp white wine vinegar to a saucepan and bring to a boil. Crack the eggs open and slide them into oiled cups. Whisk the simmering water to create a vortex. Slide the eggs in one by one, catch their movement with a large spoon to keep the egg whites around the yolks as they set. Poach the eggs gently in the simmering water for 3–4 minutes. Carefully lift from the water and season lightly with salt and pepper.

Remove the garlic from the vinaigrette. Drizzle the lettuce with the vinaigrette and serve with the bacon, croutons and poached eggs.

MUSIC: *"Adrienne Pauly", the 2006 debut album by the eponymous French actor and singer, is formidable: all nouvelle chanson without even a hint of cuteness. Adrienne Pauly's music is close to Catherine Ringer's (Les Rita Mitsouko), whose superhit "Marcia Baila" she covered for a nouvelle vague sampler series that is also very soothing as the sun goes down.*

— À VOTRE SANTÉ!! —

This matches best with a light, fruity Côtes-de-Provence rosé or a spicy Entre-Deux-Mers from Bordelais.

NON-ALCOHOLIC cider is another good choice.

SAUCISSONS EN BRIOCHE

INGREDIENTS

(makes 12 brioches)

80 g (⅓ cup) butter

125 ml (½ cup) milk

1 sugar cube

½ cube yeast (20 g)

500 g (3⅓ cups) flour (type 405),
    plus a little extra for dusting

5 g salt

2 eggs

3 thick, ideally somewhat coarse
    cooked sausages (300 g)

1 egg yolk

1 tbsp cream

Bouchées are small bites commonly served around dusk in France: savoury snacks, canapés or little pastries served with an aperitif. Saucissons en brioche are France's formidable take on sausage rolls.

————

For the brioche dough, melt the butter and leave to cool to lukewarm. Gently warm the milk and sugar and dissolve the yeast in the mixture. Combine the flour and salt in a mixing bowl. Lightly beat the eggs and add to the flour together with the remaining ingredients. Knead until glossy in a food processor, about 5 minutes. Cover the dough and set aside for 2 hours.

Quarter the sausages. Shape the dough into 12 balls of about 60 g each. Shape the remaining dough into 12 marble-sized balls. Flatten the larger balls slightly, press 1 piece of sausage in the centre, seal the dough on top and shape into a ball again. Cover with a clean dish towel and leave to rise for 30 minutes.

Preheat the oven to 200°C (390°F). Press the small balls gently on top of the larger ones and transfer the brioches to a tray lined with baking paper. Whisk the egg yolks and cream until smooth and brush the brioches with the egg wash. Bake in the preheated oven for 20–25 minutes. Serve warm or cold.

MUSIC: *Catherine Ringer, one of the grandes dames of French music who innovated French chansons in the 80s with her band Les Rita Mitsouko, recorded the live album "Les Rita Mitsouko en Concert avec l'Orchestre Lamoureux" in 2004. The song "Écoutez la chanson bien douce" and the Charles Trenet classic "Où sont-ils donc" are outstanding.*

À VOTRE SANTÉ!

Floc de Gascogne, a grape liqueur fortified with Armagnac, comes from south-western France. For a refreshing aperitif, mix 60 ml chilled red Floc de Gascogne with tonic water to taste in a tumbler and serve garnished with a slice of orange.

NON-ALCOHOLIC: pink grapefruit lemonade with tonic water and mint on ice.

GALETTE

INGREDIENTS

(makes 6 galettes)

50 g (⅓ cup) flour (type 405)

200 g (1⅓ cup) buckwheat flour

Salt

50 g (3½ tbsp) butter

2 eggs (large, plus 1 extra egg
    if cooking in a frying pan)

Oil for frying

200–250 g (2–2½ cups) grated
    tasty cheese, e.g. Gruyère

6 eggs (small)

12 thin slices of good ham

For centuries, galettes were one of the staple dishes of Breton cooking. The buckwheat for the flour grew even on the poor soils of inner Brittany, and since galettes were not considered bread, people additionally saved on taxes. Galettes were originally baked on flat stones heated in a coal fire. Even today, the savoury *pâté à galettes de blé noir* is one of the region's most popular dishes, especially the version with ham, egg and cheese.

———————

Combine the flour and buckwheat flour and add salt. Melt the butter and whisk the large eggs. Add the eggs and 100 ml (⅓ cup) water to the flour in a mixing bowl and combine to a batter with the dough hooks of a food processor or electric mixer. Gradually add the melted butter in a steady stream. This batter is now suitable for spreading on a hot crêpe cooking plate. If you intend to prepare the galettes in a frying pan, add another egg and about 125 ml (½ cup) water. Cover the batter and set aside to rest and mature for 2 hours.

Preheat the oven to 80°C (175°F) and warm the plates. Heat a large non-stick pan over medium heat and brush thinly with oil. Add 1 ladleful of batter to the pan and spread into a large pancake with the back of a spoon. Sprinkle with cheese. Crack 1 small egg and slide into the centre of the galette, spreading the egg white around. Place 2 slices of ham around the egg. Once the egg whites begin to set, fold in the sides of the galette to make a square. Transfer to a warmed plate from the oven and serve. Bake a total of 6 galettes in this way.

MUSIC: *Les Négresses Vertes and their milestone 1988 album "Mlah" are still great and very cheerful summer music, with rock-infused chansons, smoky voices, powerful beats and brass, a touch of tango, flamenco and waltz.*

—————— À VOTRE SANTÉ! ——————

Galettes are traditionally served with farmhouse cider (cidre fermier), either sweet (doux), semi-dry (demi-sec) or dry (brut), but always well chilled from a bolée, an earthenware bowl or cup.

NON-ALCOHOLIC ciders are a good alternative.

NETHERLANDS

Bitterballen are small, scrumptious croquettes with a creamy
filling; a Dutch classic that is often served with digestive bitters
or Jenever. They are currently experiencing a renaissance
as trendy street food served with an after-work beer.

BITTERBALLEN CROQUETTES

INGREDIENTS

(makes 24 briouats)

1 onion

100 g (⅓ cup) butter

150 g (1 cup) flour

700 ml (2¾ cups) beef stock

200 g corned beef

2 tbsp chopped parsley

Salt

Nutmeg

Freshly ground black pepper

Flour for breading

Eggs for breading

Breadcrumbs for breading

Plenty of oil for deep-frying

In the Amsterdam Foodhallen, I tried five different flavours of these croquettes, created and prepared by Michelin-starred chef Peter Gast, including exotic ones such as tom kha gai and bouillabaisse. Amazing! Yet, nothing's better than the original, for which you'll find the recipe here.

————

Peel and finely dice the onion. Heat the butter in a saucepan until foamy and cook the onion until translucent. Quickly whisk in the flour. Keep stirring until the mixture comes together in a thick mass. Gradually whisk in the beef stock in an even, slow stream. Mash the corned beef with a fork and also stir into the mixture. Add the chopped parsley and season with a little salt, a pinch of nutmeg and pepper.

Transfer the heavy, thick sauce to a deep tray or a baking dish. Leave to cool, cover and refrigerate for 3–4 hours until completely set.

Lightly beat the eggs. Slice the bitterballen mixture into about 48 teaspoon-sized cubes (about 20 g each). Carefully lift out of the tray or dish, shape into small balls and turn in the flour. Turn in the eggs and then in the breadcrumbs. Press the breading in gently. Transfer the balls onto plates and refrigerate until the oil is hot.

Heat oil in a deep fryer according to the manufacturer's instructions. Alternatively heat the oil in a tall saucepan to 190°C (375°F).* Deep-fry the croquettes in batches until golden brown, about 5–6 pieces per batch. Drain on kitchen paper.

* If you do not have a cooking thermometer, test with a wooden spoon: Dip the spoon handle into the hot oil. The temperature is right if small bubbles start to rise quickly.

FRIES

The Dutch are simply mad about fries and have reached similar heights in the art of making them as the world's biggest French fries nation, Belgium. In the Netherlands, fries are often served with generous sides such as creamy frietsaus (sauce for fries) and/or curry ketchup, plus freshly sliced raw onions if you ask for friet speciaal. Sheer delight.

FRIET (serves 2–4)

Peel 400 g large, waxy potatoes and slice into fries about 5–8 cm long and 1 cm thick. Rinse thoroughly in cold water to remove excess starch and pat dry between sheets of kitchen paper. Heat **oil** to 150°C (300°F) in a deep fryer according to the manufacturers' instructions. Precook the fries in batches for 5–6 minutes – they are not supposed to take on colour at this stage! Leave to cool on a baking tray. Increase the heat in the deep fryer to 175°C (345°F) and deep-fry the fries in batches until golden brown, about 3–5 minutes per batch.* Remove, season with **salt** and serve hot.

* If you do not have a cooking thermometer, test with a wooden spoon: Dip the spoon handle into the hot oil. The temperature is right if small bubbles start to rise quickly.

FRIET SPECIAAL – THE SIDES (serves 4)

Whisk 150 g (⅔ cup) mayonnaise, 1 tsp tomato paste, ½ tsp hot mustard and **1 pinch paprika powder** until smooth. Season with **1 dash tarragon vinegar, salt** and piment **d'Espelette**. Peel and finely dice **1 small red onion** and also season with 1 dash tarragon vinegar and salt. Finely slice some **spring onions** and sprinkle over the fries together with the diced onion and sauce.

PROOST!

Jenever, a predecessor of gin, is the national beverage of the Dutch. From about five pm (an excellent time for a golden hour), people gather for a borreltje (a small glass) of Jenever with a touch of Angostura bitters. Depending on your company, this may soon turn into a borreluur, an entire hour (or more) of gregariousness.

CRISPY ONION RINGS WITH A HERB & SOUR CREAM DIP

The Netherlands have a rich culture of snack foods, and typically Dutch snack bars serve a wide range of deep-fried delicacies, including crispy onion rings, a dish that has everything it takes to become a new cocktail hour favourite.

CRISPY ONION RINGS (serves 2–4)

Peel 1 mild onion and slice into rings. Turn in **2 tbsp flour**. Combine **30 g semolina** with **50 g breadcrumbs** and season with **1 pinch piment d'Espelette**. Use a fork to dip the onion rings first into **50 ml (¼ cup) buttermilk** and then turn them in the breadcrumb mixture. Heat **oil** to 175°C (345°F) in a deep fryer according to the manufacturers' instructions.* Fry the onion rings in batches until golden brown. Drain on kitchen paper and season with **salt**.

* If you do not have a cooking thermometer, test with a wooden spoon: Dip the spoon handle into the hot oil. The temperature is right if small bubbles start to rise quickly.

HERB & SOUR CREAM DIP (serves 2–4)

Whisk 150 g (⅔ cup) sour cream and **50 g (¼ cup) mayonnaise** with **1 tbsp horseradish cream** until smooth. Finely chop **4 sprigs dill** and **2 sprigs tarragon** and stir into the mixture. Finely chop **1 bunch chives** and add. Season with **1 dash herb vinegar** and **salt**.

MUSIC: *The 2016 album "Fading Lines" by the Dutch singer/songwriter Amber Arcades moves elegantly and playfully between melancholy pop ("This Time") and pulsating electronica ("Turning Light"). Simply great!*

PROOST!

How about a **Red Jenever**? Stir **20 ml Jenever** or gin with **20 ml red vermouth**, **50 ml cold red grape juice** and **3 ice cubes** in a mixer glass and strain into a chilled tumbler.

NON-ALCOHOLIC: red grape juice mixed 2:1 with Sanbittèr.

PORTUGAL

If there is such a thing as a favourite city, then mine
would be Lisbon, this colourful, creative, lovely, friendly
beauty of a city on the mouth of the Tejo river.

Lisbon is bathed in a unique light at the sundown, when a gentle breeze brings coolness to the end of the day, when there is music everywhere, when the streets and laneways are filled with laughter and people and the aromas of a myriad of little delicacies served in the city's countless open kitchens and alfresco restaurants. There are clams in wine with coriander (cilantro, p. 178), for example, or braised and oven-baked bacalhau (p. 188) and so much more, served with a sweeping view over the city's hills while the lights start coming on.

During our visit, we spent a day exploring the city in a tuk-tuk, booked a tour of the famous Alfama district and climbed the Miradouro de Santa Luzia, where we enjoyed what is probably Lisbon's best view. The next morning, we ate a still-warm pastel de nata from the Pastelaria Balcão do Marquês and a toasted ham and cheese sandwich for breakfast before we travelled on along the coast to the Alentejo region.

We booked a room with Maria in the Cabeça de Cabra, a former village primary school with its own garden. Every morning, the guests sat around a long table, savouring deliciously fresh bread, air-cured ham and local cheeses, and every morning Maria served some extras, sometimes zucchini (courgette) salad, sometimes freshly picked tomatoes from the garden or home-made pastries. There was a pasture behind the building, where happy brown cows fed on the leaves of a walnut tree. We listened to the gentle sounds of the cowbells and gave ourselves entirely over to leisure.

We drove to the coast past gently rolling hills, ancient cork oaks and sweeping fields. My image of Portugal had always been that of a dry, rocky and sunburnt place, but in July, the country's colours were earthy reds, wheaty yellows and dark greens beneath a wide blue sky dotted with white clouds. Suddenly I wished I could paint. The sea was exciting, powerful, crystal clear and refreshingly cold. We spent many days on our favourite beach, Praia Malhão, where we ate caracóis and migas à alentejana (p. 180), and our skin smelled of sea water and sun. As the shadows deepen, the A Choupana in Vila Nova de Milfontes served fresh fish and prawns straight off the BBQ. Just a few blocks further along, we ate the best clams of the entire trip at the Portinho do Canal restaurant, which cooked them in an intense broth of fish stock, garlic and plenty of bay leaves with added olive oil for creaminess. And arroz de marisco, seafood rice with pieces of crayfish, locust lobsters and small prawns cooked in an aromatic shellfish broth in a huge pot.

We travelled further south still to explore Arrifana (Aljezur), Lagos and the Algarve, knowing that we'd just have to come back to get a taste of Porto and the Douro valley.

PORTUGAL: WHERE THE STREETS ARE FILLED WITH MUSIC

SUNSET WITH A VIEW

Lisbon's seven hills are full of excellent sunset viewing points, but the most spectacular of all is the Miradouro da Graça. Just be prepared for quite a bit of company. The rugged coast and wild beaches of Arrifana (Aljezur) in southern Portugal are highly recommended. They are breathtaking at any time of the day.

AMÊIJOAS À BULHÃO PATO

Clams with garlic & coriander

In my mind, this dish, which is named after the Portuguese poet and bon vivant Raimundo António de Bulhão (1828–1912), embodies everything that is typical of good Portuguese cooking: just a few high-quality ingredients, generously portioned, turn even the simplest of clam stews into a culinary discovery. The delicate clam flavour is the clear hero of the dish, beautifully presented in a richly aromatic broth with depth from garlic and olive oil and freshness from fragrant lemon and fresh coriander (cilantro, a firm favourite of Portuguese cuisine). Perfection.

HERE'S HOW (serves 4)

WASH **1 kg clams** in cold water and discard any that are already open. Peel and finely slice **4 garlic cloves**. Heat **80 ml (4 tbsp) olive oil** in a large saucepan, add the garlic and fry until translucent, stirring continuously. Add half of **1 bunch coriander** in its entirety. Add half of **300 ml (1¼ cups) white wine** and bring to a boil. Add the remaining wine and return to a boil. Add the clams, season with **salt** and stir. Cover and simmer for 4 minutes, then remove the clams from the broth with a slotted spoon and transfer to a warmed bowl. Cover and keep warm. Add the **juice of 1 lemon** to the broth and simmer uncovered to reduce for 6–8 minutes. Chop the remaining coriander. Pour the broth over the clams, sprinkle with the chopped coriander and drizzle with a little fresh olive oil.

MUSIC: *The impossibilities of love! Fado is an expression of unfathomable longing, wistfulness, passion, melancholy, a desire to be elsewhere. This is the music of Portugal and the Portuguese soul. Amália Rodrigues, one of Portugal's national icons, is considered the queen of fado, and while she died in 1999, a number of very strong fadistas are continuing her legacy. We recommend Carminho and Mariza, or Ana Moura, whose 2012 album "Desfado" combines traditional fado music with jazz elements.*

SAÚDE!

Enjoy with a Vinho Verde.

NON-ALCOHOLIC: try iced lemon and ginger tea.

MIGAS À ALENTEJANA

Bread omelette

INGREDIENTS

(serves 4)

**300 g light sourdough bread
or cornbread**

2 onions

2–3 garlic cloves

5 tbsp olive oil, plus some extra

1 tsp sweet paprika powder

Chilli to taste

Salt

**About 300–450 ml (1½–2½ cups)
strong beef stock (alternatively
vegetable stock)**

3 eggs (medium-sized)

4 sprigs flat-leaf parsley

½ bunch coriander (cilantro)

This Alentejo dish is a delicious way of using up leftovers: migas (breadcrumbs) from stale bread are cooked to a porridge consistency with stock, onions and garlic, then fried to make an "omelette" and served with fresh coriander. I first had this hybrid between a dumpling and an omelette from the Alentejo region in the town of Porto Covo together with a cold beer and a plate of caracóis, tiny snails in a garlic broth. Amazing!

———

Pulse the bread in a food processor to make coarse crumbs. Peel the onion and garlic. Mince the garlic and finely dice the onion. Heat the oil in a large non-stick frying pan. Add the onion and garlic and sauté until soft. Add the bread, dust with paprika powder and a touch of chilli and season with salt. Next, stir in some stock: the amount will depend on the bread used. The idea is to have the breadcrumbs soften to make a dough-like, firm porridge within a few minutes.

Push the bread mixture together to form a loaf. Add a little more olive oil to the pan and continue frying. Serve as a side dish – in the Alentejo this is eaten with ribs or BBQ meats. Alternatively, make finger food migas by transferring the porridge to a bowl, quickly stirring in the eggs, one by one, and spreading the dough out in a baking dish. Preheat the oven to 200°C (390°F) and bake for 15–20 minutes on the middle rack. Remove and set aside to rest for 10 minutes. Chop the parsley and coriander and sprinkle over the migas. Slice and serve warm or cold.

MUSIC: *The Lisbon band Orelha Negra samples Portuguese and Latin American sounds and blends them with electronic, funk, soul and hip-hop music. Worth listening: their debut album "Orelha Negra" (2010).*

SAÚDE!

Serve with chilled white port or Vinho Verde.

NON-ALCOHOLIC: chilled green grape juice on ice, flavoured with fresh mint and organic orange zest.

TWO TYPES OF
FISH SALADS FROM LISBON

Portuguese specialties include tinned sardines (sardinha), tuna and bacalhau (dried cod) in exquisite olive oil, chilli oil, smoked oil or any number of sauces and seasonings. Among them are sardines millésimées – genuine vintage sardines matured in tins.

High-quality produce and careful processing make these tinned fish varieties true delicacies, plus the tins are often works of art in themselves. Empty tins therefore make lovely serving dishes for home-made fish salad, as seen for example in one of the countless street bars on Lisbon's Avenida da Liberdade, a magnificent boulevard lined with palm and plantain trees. If you're lucky, you may even experience locals coming together here for a weekend dance under the evening sky.

BACALHAU & CHICKPEA SALAD
(serves 2–4)

Drain **1 tin chickpeas (425 g net weight)** and transfer the chickpeas to a bowl. Peel **1 onion**, slice finely and add to the bowl. Marinate with **2–3 tbsp white wine vinegar** and **4 tbsp olive oil** and season with **salt** and **freshly ground black pepper**. Pull **150 g cooked bacalhau** (recipe p. 188 or from a tin) into bite-sized pieces and toss with the marinade. Dust the salad with **sweet paprika powder** before serving.

TUNA & BEAN SALAD (serves 2–4)

Drain **1 tin white beans (425 g net weight)** and transfer the beans to a bowl. Peel **1 red onion**, dice finely and add to the bowl. Marinate with the **juice of ½ lemon** and **4 tbsp olive oil** and season with **salt** and **cayenne pepper**. Chop **4 sprigs parsley**, pull **150 g tuna in brine** into bite-sized pieces and toss both with the marinade.

—— SAÚDE! ——

Until quite recently, Portugal only had Super Bock and sagres beers, but the country now has an emerging craft beer movement. A chilled, lemony Urraca Vendaval, an Indian pale ale made by the Lisbon micro-brewery Oitava Colina, goes very well with fish salad and a sunset.

1 Oven-baked bacalhau
2 Pan-fried bacalhau
3 Maionese de bacalhau
4 Bolinhos de bacalhau

BACALHAU

Portuguese dried cod

Bacalhau is a national treasure of Portuguese cuisine. An old saying has it that Portugal has 1001 recipes for salted, dried cod. It might not actually be that many, but certainly there is at least one for each day of the year. Dried cod originated in Norway, but Portuguese seafarers brought it back home, and it gradually became a popular dish for lent as well as an important commodity and part of Portuguese culture.

SOAK THE BACALHAU

Rinse **1 kg bacalhau**, cut into pieces along the bones, under cold water. Transfer to a container with a lid, cover with cold water and refrigerate. Keep soaking for 5–6 days. Change the water initially every 6–8 hours, then two to three times every 24 hours. Cut the flesh from the bones and continue to process.

BACALHAU FISH STOCK

The bones make a very flavourful fish stock!

———

Transfer the **bones** to a saucepan and cover with fresh, cold water. Trim, wash and dice **1 bunch soup vegetables** and add to the saucepan. Crush **2 ripe tomatoes** and **1 garlic clove**, halve **2 unpeeled onions** and also add, together with **1 tsp mustard seeds**, **2 bay leaves** and **150 ml (⅔ cup) white wine**. Slowly bring to a boil, then reduce the heat and simmer the stock for 20 minutes. Carefully strain through a sieve lined with a muslin cloth and season with **salt**. Use straight away or freeze in portion sizes.

OVEN-BAKED BACALHAU (serves 4)

One of the easiest bacalhau recipes. The clarity of its flavours really allows the fish to shine.

———

Preheat the oven to 220°C (430°F). Peel **1 small red onion** and slice finely. Thinly slice **4 small tomatoes** and season lightly with **salt**. Peel and finely slice **1 garlic clove**. Heat **8 tbsp olive oil** in a large pan. Add **2 bay leaves**, the onion and garlic and sauté for 2–3 minutes. Season **400–500 g bacalhau fillet** with **3–4 tbsp lemon juice**. Transfer to a baking dish, top with the sliced tomatoes and cooked onions, season with **pepper** and bake in the preheated oven for 10–12 minutes. Serve garnished with a few fresh **sprigs of coriander (cilantro)**.

PAN-FRIED BACALHAU (serves 4)

This even easier recipe foregrounds the cod flavour. Its exquisite balance of spice, acidity and salt matches perfectly with chilled Vinho Verde and green olives.

———

Separate **400–500 g bacalhau fillets** into pieces. Rub with **1 tbsp lemon juice** and **1 tbsp white wine**. Combine **4 tbsp flour** and **1 tsp cornflour (cornstarch)** and turn the fish pieces in the mixture. Heat a generous amount of basic **olive oil** in a frying pan and fry the fish 4–6 minutes on each side. Serve with **lemon** and a little **sea salt**.

MAIONESE DE BACALHAU (serves 4–6)

I first ate maionese de raia, an incredibly creamy, richly flavoured mash of potatoes and mayonnaise with pulled skate fillet, in the bar A Tasca do kiko in the port of Lagos. This is the bacalhau version.

———

Peel and dice **600 g floury potatoes** and boil in **salted water** until soft. Drain and set aside to cool. Bring **250 ml (1 cup) fish stock** to a boil, add **250 g bacalhau** and simmer gently over low heat for 8 minutes. Remove and leave to cool. Slice **1 spring onion** into rings and separate the green and white parts. Transfer the potatoes and fish to a bowl. Add **80 g (⅓ cup) mayonnaise**, **1 minced clove garlic**, **1 pinch grated lemon zest** and **1 tsp lemon juice**. Stir in the white spring onion slices, season lightly with salt and stir with a fork to combine, adding spoonfuls of fish stock until you get a creamy texture. Serve sprinkled with green spring onion rings.

BOLINHOS DE BACALHAU (serves 4)

These are one of the most popular Portuguese petiscos, that is finger foods to have with an aperitif.

———

The day before, cook **350 g floury potatoes** in their skins. Leave to cool and rest overnight. Bring **250 ml (1 cup) fish stock** to a boil, add **250 g bacalhau** and simmer over low heat for 8 minutes. Remove and leave to cool. Peel and dice the potatoes. Pull the fish into very small pieces and add to the potatoes. Crush **1 garlic clove**, finely chop **a few sprigs of flat-leaf parsley** and add together with **1 egg**. Season with **salt**, **1 pinch grated nutmeg** and a little **cayenne pepper** and knead to a homogeneous dough. Heat **oil for deep-frying** to about 180°C (350°F) in a saucepan or deep fryer.* Use a tablespoon dipped in water to form small quenelles and deep-fry for 2–3 minutes each.

* If you do not have a cooking thermometer, test with a wooden spoon: Dip the spoon handle into the hot oil. The temperature is right if small bubbles start to rise quickly.

SARDINES ON RAISIN TOAST

with tomato and passionfruit chutney

INGREDIENTS

(makes 8 toasts)

1 onion

8 tbsp olive oil

1 tsp raw sugar

2 tomatoes

1 tsp white wine vinegar

Salt

2 passionfruit

4 slices raisin bread

Butter for spreading

24 small, fresh anchovy fillets
   (may need to be pre-ordered
   from your fishmonger)

Flour for breading

Lisbon! The famous funicular Ascensor da Glória creakily climbs the equally famous Calçada da Glória every day and has done so since 1885. It carries us up to the magnificent park Jardim de São Pedro de Alcântara, where we enjoy freshly squeezed, chilled orange juice and lemon and ginger lemonade with a panoramic view of the city that opens our hearts. Closer to sunset, we stroll across the road to the Insólito, a rooftop restaurant and bar, again with a beautiful view of the city. The restaurant is accessed via Lisbon's oldest (and most likely tiniest) lift, but this test of courage is well worth it. This is where I enjoyed the sardine toasts that were the inspiration for the following recipe.

———————

Peel and finely dice the onion. Heat 3 tbsp olive oil in a frying pan and cook until soft, about 4–6 minutes. Add the sugar and stir to dissolve. Quarter the tomatoes, deseed, dice and stir into the softened onions. Season with vinegar and salt and remove from the heat. Halve the passionfruit, spoon out the pulp and stir into the mixture. Leave the chutney to cool slightly.

Halve the raisin toast slices and toast. Spread thinly with butter. Press the skin side of the anchovy fillets into the flour and shake off any excess. Heat 5 tbsp olive oil in a large non-stick pan and fry the fillets on the skin side only for 1–2 minutes. Season lightly with salt. Divide the warm chutney and anchovy fillets on the slices of toast. Serve immediately.

MUSIC: *On the night we visited, the Insólito played relaxed trip-hop from the 90s. Recommended listening: "Who Can You Trust" (1996) by Morcheeba and "Blue Lines" (1991) by Massive Attack.*

— SAÚDE! —

A perfect match: port & tonic. Pour white port over ice cubes in a tumbler glass and top with chilled tonic water at a ratio of 1:2. Garnish with lemon zest.

NON-ALCOHOLIC: use green grape juice instead of the port.

PASTÉIS DE NATA

INGREDIENTS

(makes 12, one large muffin tray)

50 g (3½ cups) butter, softened,
   plus a little extra for the tin

450 g puff pastry, defrosted

1 vanilla pod

500 ml (2 cups) milk

5 egg yolks (from medium-sized
   eggs)**

1 egg

50 g (⅓ cup) flour

250 g (1¼ cups) sugar

2 pinches finely grated lemon zest
   (best organic)

1 pinch cinnamon

Salt

Raw sugar, for dusting

Lisbon's best-known pastries are popular all over the world. However, most of the commercially available, usually cold and tough custard-filled puff pastry tarts really lack the love and attention that makes the original so special. Not so in Lisbon, where the tarts are served warm, fresh out of the oven, with a featherlight, crisp pastry. Even the custard is still warm, and when you order the tarts at a bakery, you'll get them dusted with cinnamon if you like, which tastes sensational. Many think the Confeitaria Pastéis de Belém, R. Belém 84–92, makes the best Portuguese tarts, but I also love the ones from Pastelaria Balcão do Marquês, Av. Duque de Loulé 113. Here's my recipe, though, in case you can't get there.

———

Brush the moulds of a muffin tray thinly with softened butter. Cut 12 circles of about 10 cm diameter from the puff pastry.* Line the moulds with the circles and refrigerate the tray.

Slice the vanilla open lengthwise and scrape out the seeds. Add the seeds and pod to the milk, along with the egg yolk, egg, butter, flour, sugar, lemon zest, cinnamon and a pinch of salt. Bring to a boil, whisking continually. Remove from the heat and leave to cool a little.

Preheat the oven to 220°C (430°F). Divide the custard among the moulds and bake in the preheated oven for 15 minutes. Sprinkle the tops with raw sugar and continue to bake for another 4–6 minutes. Leave to rest briefly in the tray, then unmould and leave to cool on a wire rack.

* Knead puff pastry offcuts together, roll out and dust with icing sugar or a little grated cheese. Bake in the preheated oven (220°C / 430°F) for 12–15 minutes to make little nibblies.

** Use the 5 egg whites to make meringues: Use an electric mixer to whisk the egg whites until stiff. Gradually incorporate the sugar. Transfer the mixture to a piping bag and pipe rings, rosettes or small balls onto a tray lined with baking paper. Bake at 120°C (250°F) for about 1 hour.

— SAÚDE! —

Serve warm with coffee or a small glass
of port wine. Or both.

UNITED KINGDOM

The development of my musical tastes is entirely shaped
by British influences. Even the first music that I graduated
to from cassettes of fairy tales and children's music were
my mother's Beatles records.

Later, I translated the lyrics word by word with a dictionary. At various stages of my life, I most closely identified with Ringo (nobody loves me) or John (love, peace, middle finger). The Beatles then led me straight on to the Neue Deutsche Welle, ska and punk, Madness, The Selecter, the Sex Pistols and The Clash.

I felt sorry for myself over albums by The Smith, discovered wave and electronic music with Depeche Mode and The Cure, and British dub and jungle with Adrian Sherwood and Mad Professor. The heroes of my youth were Ray Cokes and David Rodigan, and I just kept listening to new music from the UK: Blur, Tricky, Massive Attack, Fatboy Slim. Such talent! It certainly wasn't the food that attracted me, as a first visit to London in the 80s proved to be rather disillusioning. The sausages actually tasted of sawdust, but the curries were ok and Chinese food was good and cheap.

And then came Jamie Oliver. He conquered TV screens everywhere in his sneakers, colourful print shirts and skull hoodies – confident, cocky and authentic. His recipes were of an ingenious simplicity. At the time, I was already a fully qualified chef and deeply impressed. Jamie blew the dust off British cooking, uncovered forgotten treasures, and taught the Brits that cooking is fun and food can actually taste good. In the process, he also breathed new life into classic bar food. In the UK, sundown means a visit to the pub, with a fluid transition between bar snacks and dinner, with steak pie (p. 197), fish & chips and Scotch eggs (p. 202).

A new generation of British chefs is proud of their culinary heritage, whose richness and diversity are closely connected to the country's colonial and migration history. London has pioneering trend-setters such as Fergus Henderson (St. John Bread & Wine), who launched the nose-to-tail revolution, or Yotam Ottolenghi (Nopi), who made eastern Mediterranean cooking a worldwide trend with his relaxed recipes and Oriental flavours. The city has become an epicentre of new culinary developments and innovation, and it is very much the countless foodies, farmers, culinary start-ups and small restaurants that make British cuisine so amazing. Plus they have great music...

HAGGIS MEATBALLS

with apple and cranberry sauce

INGREDIENTS

(serves 4–6)

For the meat balls:

50 g (¼ cup) pearl barley

Salt

100 g cooked beef tongue, sliced

1 onion

20 g butter

100 g veal liver

500 g minced beef

20 g ginger

6 sprigs marjoram (alternatively
1 tsp dried marjoram)

Nutmeg

1 pinch each ground allspice and
coriander (cilantro)

Freshly ground black pepper

1 bunch flat-leaf parsley

30 g (¼ cup) breadcrumbs

1 egg (large)

Oil

For the sauce:

6–8 tbsp stewed apples

4–6 tbsp cranberries

2–3 tsp chilli sauce

Salt

SLÁINTE!

Enjoy this with a Scottish beer, ideally dark
and malty, or with a Scotch whisky.

NON-ALCOHOLIC: tomato juice
seasoned with a little salt and pepper and
a dash of pickle juice.

Every January 25th, Scotland celebrates *Burns Night* in honour of Robert Burns, the Scottish poet and national hero, who was born on that day in 1759. An essential part of any *Burns supper* is haggis, sheep's stomach stuffed with chopped offal, suet, onions and oatmeal. While this may not sound very tempting to non-Scots, it is in fact delicious if you give it a go. Of course, haggis is also served in pubs, and I hope that haggis meatballs are a gentle introduction to this often-underappreciated dish. The meatball recipe below comes close to the flavour of the original but does so without the suet and sheep's stomach. Haggis for beginners, essentially. May it entice you to try out the genuine thing next January 25th!

Haggis is traditionally served while diners take turns reciting Robert Burns poems, including his most famous, the "Address to a Haggis": *Fair fa' your honest, sonsie face, Great Chieftain o' the Puddin-race! ...* We only say, sláinte!

Rinse the pearl barley thoroughly under cold water, then boil in salted water for 30 minutes. Finely dice the beef tongue. Halve and finely dice the onion. Heat the butter in a frying pan, sauté both and leave to cool. Mince the veal liver very finely and add to the beef mince together with the diced beef tongue and onions. Season with freshly grated ginger, chopped marjoram and a pinch of nutmeg, allspice, ground coriander and black pepper. Chop the parsley and add to the meat mixture. Stir in the breadcrumbs and egg. Drain the barley and refresh under cold water. Add to the mixture. Season with salt and knead to a smooth dough with an electric mixer. Cover and set aside to rest for 20 minutes.

→ Read on overleaf

Meanwhile, whisk the cranberries and chilli sauce into the stewed apples and season with a pinch of salt. Shape the meat mixture into bite-sized balls. Heat a little oil in a non-stick pan and fry the balls until golden brown, about 8–10 minutes. Serve warm or cold with the apple and cranberry dip.

MUSIC: *A perfect occasion for listening to Glasgow band Belle & Sebastian's 2003 album "Dear Catastrophe Waitress", produced by Trevor Horn. Light but never fluffy Scottish guitar pop.*

STEAK PIE

INGREDIENTS

(serves 4–6)

500 g (3⅓ cups) flour (type 405, plus extra for the dish)

200 g (¾ cup) butter, at room temperature (plus extra for the dish)

50 g (3½ tbsp) ghee (plus extra for frying)

2 eggs (medium-sized)

Salt

1 tsp vinegar

800 g streaky beef for stew

200 g onions

20 g dried mushrooms (ceps or mixed)

1 tbsp tomato paste

1 tsp raw sugar

2 sprigs thyme

8 juniper berries, lightly crushed

These mini pies filled with juicy braised beef are very popular in the United Kingdom, both as a family dinner and as pub food. For the bar version, I've added a little brown ale to the stew, which creates a delicious flavour.

Combine the flour, butter, ghee, eggs, 5 g salt, 2 tsp water and vinegar to a crumbly dough in a food processor. Do not overmix. Transfer to your benchtop and quickly knead into a smooth dough. Shape into 12 balls and refrigerate for 20 minutes. Brush the moulds of a muffin tray with a little butter and dust with flour. Refrigerate.

Meanwhile, cut the beef into small dice about 0.5–1 cm in size. Peel and finely dice the onions. Heat a little ghee in a casserole dish over high heat. Add the meat and onion and sear in batches. Pulse the dried mushrooms in a food processor until finely chopped. Return all the meat and onions to the casserole dish and stir in the tomato paste and dried mushrooms. Sprinkle with raw sugar, season with salt and pepper and stir in the thyme, juniper and bay leaves.

→ Please turn over

STEAK PIE *continued*

2 bay leaves

Freshly ground black pepper

300 ml brown ale

400 ml (1½ cups) beef stock

Brown gravy powder

Pour over the beer and simmer, uncovered, for 3 minutes. Add the stock, cover and braise gently for 1 hour 15 minutes.

Thicken the beef stew with 1–2 tsp brown gravy powder and leave to cool. Remove the bay leaves and thyme.

Divide each dough ball into 2 pieces, one twice the size of the other. Roll out the pieces; use the larger ones for lining the muffin moulds and reserve the smaller ones for the pie lids. Refrigerate the muffin tray lined with the dough.

Preheat the oven to 200°C (390°F). Use a tablespoon to divide the cooled beef stew among the muffin moulds (any leftover stew makes a fabulous pasta sauce!) and cover with the lids. Press the edges together to seal. Pierce the tops with a fork in the centre. Transfer the muffin tray to the preheated oven and bake for 25–30 minutes on the lowest rack. Serve warm.

MUSIC: *In 1993, the London band Us3 published a milestone album of dancefloor jazz, a genre that was hugely popular at the time: their mastermind Geoff Wilkinson sampled jazz classics from the archive of the legendary Blue Note Records label for his "Hand on the Torch" album, combining them with hip-hop elements to create hits such as "Cantaloop (Flip Fantasia)" and "Tukka Yoot's Riddim". A first-rate classic for any golden hour.*

CHEERS!

Who could go past a Guinness with these!

NON-ALCOHOLIC: serve ginger ale with fresh cucumber slices and a slice of orange on ice; alternatively chilled herb lemonade.

CHICKEN TIKKA MASALA

INGREDIENTS

(serves 4–6)

1 uncooked chicken (about 1 kg)

2 tsp garam masala (alternatively curry powder)

150 g (½ cup) Greek yoghurt

1 red bullhorn capsicum

3 tomatoes

200 g onions

2 tbsp ghee

2 garlic cloves

20 g ginger

1 star anise (optional)

1 pinch cinnamon

1 tsp turmeric

1 tbsp sweet paprika powder

2 tbsp honey

1–2 pinches sambal oelek (optional)

1 tin diced tomatoes
(425 g net weight)

400 ml (1½ cups) chicken stock

1 level tsp cornflour (cornstarch)

Salt

1 tsp toasted black sesame seeds
(optional)

A few fresh sprigs of coriander

CHEERS!

Enjoy this with a British beer: a lager, Indian pale ale, porter or imperial stout.

NON-ALCOHOLIC: chicken tikka masala is great with a refreshing lassi. Blend plain yoghurt with a little fresh cucumber and a touch of salt.

The Brits acquired a truly exotic national dish through their seafaring and colonial history: chicken tikka masala (masala = mixed spices). In India, chicken tikka are spicy chicken skewers cooked over coal in a tandoor oven. The creamy tomato sauce served with this dish is a British addition, though – they like their gravy in the UK, after all.

Separate the chicken: cut the wings and thighs; cut the breast off the bone. Divide the breast into thirds; halve the thigh at the joint. Cut the remaining carcass into pieces with poultry shears. Transfer to a saucepan and cover with water. Bring to a boil and simmer gently for 20 minutes. Strain the liquid through a sieve to make a light chicken stock.

Whisk the garam masala into 1 tbsp of the yoghurt and rub the mixture into the chicken pieces. Coarsely dice the capsicum and tomatoes. Peel and coarsely dice the onions. Heat the ghee in a casserole dish. Add the meat, capsicum and tomatoes and fry until everything starts to take on colour. Meanwhile, peel and mince the garlic. Peel and finely grate the ginger. Add the ginger, garlic, star anise, cinnamon, turmeric and paprika powder to the meat.

Stir in the honey and sambal oelek, if using, and add the diced tomatoes and the chicken stock. Cover and simmer gently over medium heat for about 20 minutes. Remove the lid and reduce for another 20 minutes. Whisk the cornflour into the remaining yoghurt, then return the mixture to the tomato stew until it thickens a little. Season with salt. Garnish with toasted black sesame seeds and fresh coriander leaves to serve.

SERVE WITH basmati rice and red lentils or plain flatbread or naan bread.

MUSIC: *Amy Winehouse's posthumously published album "Lioness: Hidden Treasures" (2011). We still miss her.*

SCOTCH EGGS

One of the greatest bar foods of all times comes from the British Isles: Scotch eggs, that is soft-boiled or medium eggs, wrapped in a layer of well-seasoned mince and coated with crisp breading – just divine. However, this recipe didn't actually originate in Scotland, but in North Africa, where British seafarers came to love spicy eggs seasoned with whole cloves and brought the recipe back to the UK. A similar recipe is also found in India, where eggs coated in fried mutton mince and served in an onion and tomato sauce were known as nargisi kofta well before deep-frying as a cooking technique was even known in the UK.

The first reference to Scotch eggs in England comes from late 19th century Whitby, North Yorkshire, where William J. Scott & Sons sold eggs coated in fish paste and breading. Their recipe was very successful, and they wanted to sell it further afield, so they replaced the creamy fish paste by a firmer minced beef coating to be able to transport the eggs. Scotch eggs are traditionally served with a tangy yoghurt and mayonnaise dip. Be warned – they are addictive.

HERE'S HOW (makes 4 eggs, can be scaled up easily)

Boil **4 eggs** (**small** ones; large eggs make the recipe difficult) for 4–5 minutes. Refresh in cold water and peel. Carefully wrap the eggs in a coat of 80 g mince each (i.e. **320 g mince** altogether). Whisk **1 medium-sized egg**. Turn the coated eggs in **4 tbsp flour (type 405)** and shake off any excess. Turn first in the whisked egg and then in about **150 g (1⅓ cups) breadcrumbs**. Press the breading in well. Heat **plenty of oil** in a deep fryer according to the manufacturers' instructions. Alternatively heat the oil in a tall saucepan to 160–170°C (320–340°F).* Deep-fry the eggs in the hot oil until golden brown, about 8–10 minutes. Drain on kitchen paper.

CHIVES DIP (serves 4)

Whisk **200 g** (¾ **cup) sour cream** or **heavy sour cream** with **2 tbsp pickle juice**, **1 dash herb vinegar** and **1 pea-sized amount of wasabi** (alternatively ½ tsp hot mustard) until smooth. Season with **salt**.

* If you do not have a cooking thermometer, test with a wooden spoon: Dip the spoon handle into the hot oil. The temperature is right if small bubbles start to rise.

CHEERS!

Scotch eggs are fabulous with beer – and, of course, Scotch whisky.

MUSIC: *How about Robbie Williams and his 2001 swing album "Swing When You're Winning", which has become a true classic for any cocktail hour.*

BRAZIL

I travelled to Brazil upon an invitation by the Brazilian Goethe Institute in São Paulo and had the great privilege of presenting my books and cookbooks both at the Institute and at the Brazilian book fair. I arrived hugely curious about Brazilian cooking.

Lucky me met Daniela Narciso and Danilo Rolim, who run a catering business together and share my passion for good food. Ana Rüsche, a writer and beer sommelier, completed our group of four on our culinary excursions.

Saturdays in Brazil are *feijoada* days. This stew of black beans, salted meat, beef tongue, sausage, rice, toasted manioc flour, couve mineira cabbage, hot pimenta sauce and fresh oranges is traditionally served for lunch (Brazilians will say it gives nightmares if eaten at night). However, since I was at the book fair throughout the days, my companions kindly located a restaurant that would serve us *feijoada* in the evening, which is probably a little like asking for a cappuccino at breakfast time in an Italian bar – it instantly outs the tourist.

For my last day in the city, Daniela and Danilo took me to the Mocotó Bar e Restaurante, where Rodrigo Oliveira cooks his multi-award-winning regional food from north-eastern Brazil at the pinnacle of culinary skill. The restaurant on the outskirts of Rio is one of Brazil's best, and Oliveira is a man with a mission. He's had offers to move closer to the centre, but he's committed to staying where he is, preserving his father's heritage and looking ahead to the future, as the Mocotó trains young locals to a high standard.

In Brazil, sundown naturally starts with a freshly prepared caipirinha, the national beverage. We were given a brief introduction at the bar, which serves snacks at all sorts of times of the day, not only at dusk. There was a whole range of caipirinhas on offer, with different types of fruits, with chilli of without. Genuine caipirinha is sweetened with *açúcar de baunilha com especiarias*, a fine sugar flavoured with lightly crushed juniper berries, star anise, cardamom and vanilla pods. At that bar I understood just how delicious caipirinha (p. 210) can actually be.

It was served with a few snacks: sausage flambéed with cachaça (p. 211) and fried cheese (*queijo de coalho com melado*, p. 211). The evening then moved on to even more delicacies – the aromas from the kitchen were irresistible. That night, I was privileged to taste an authentic piece of traditional Brazilian cooking with new friends on the polished counter of the Mocotó bar. Thank you!

SALMON CEVICHE

with sweet potatoes and black beans

INGREDIENTS

(serves 4)

**300–400 g deboned fresh
salmon fillet**

2 limes

1 green chilli

Salt

1 organic Lebanese cucumber

200 g sweet potatoes

Olive oil

200 g black beans (from a tin)

1 red onion

Red wine vinegar

1 spring onion

½ bunch coriander (cilantro)

Chilli flakes

Ceviche, that is very fresh raw, marinated fish or prawns, seasoned with lime juice, onions, coriander and green chilli, has a long tradition in many coastal regions of Latin America. This Brazilian version (Brazilian salmon is mainly imported from Chile) plays on the national colours and is as refreshing as it is fiery and energising.

———

Freeze the salmon briefly for 10–15 minutes to firm it up. Cut into bite-sized pieces and marinate in the lime juice. Thinly slice the chilli and toss with the salmon. Add salt and leave to marinate for at least 30 minutes. Meanwhile, slice the cucumber, season generously with salt and set aside. Peel and dice the sweet potato. Boil in salted water for 6–8 minutes, drain and refresh under cold water. Drain again and season with salt and a little olive oil.

Drain the beans, rinse under cold water, season with salt and also toss with a little olive oil. Peel and finely dice the red onion. Season with a dash of red wine vinegar and salt. Slice the spring onion into rings. Pick off the coriander leaves and leave a few tender stems whole for garnish. Remove the salmon from the marinade and arrange on plates with the drained cucumber, sweet potato and beans. Sprinkle with the remaining ingredients and chilli flakes to taste and serve immediately.

MUSIC: *The London band Smoke City fused Brazilian samba and bossa nova rhythms with jazz and trip hop elements in the late 90s. Their 1997 album "Flying Away" is a bar classic, and the single "Underwater Love" is a perfect match for salmon.*

SAÚDE!

A light lager or fresh Indian pale ale –
ice-cold and served with a wedge of lime.

NON-ALCOHOLIC: mix passionfruit
or mango juice with sparkling mineral
water and a dash of lime juice. Serve on ice.

1 Guacamole
2 Pão de queijo
3 Queijo-de-coalho
4 Lingüiça com cebola

PÃO DE QUEIJO, GUACAMOLE WITH CAPSICUM & TOMATO SALSA

and caipirinha

Three classic bar foods that are essential for any sunset in Brazil: *pão de queijo* (airy choux pastry and cheese puffs), guacamole and an authentic caipirinha – *batida de limão*.

PÃO DE QUEIJO (makes about 35 puffs)

Bring **125 ml (½ cup) water**, **25 g (1⅔ tbsp) butter** and **1 pinch salt** to a boil in a small saucepan. Remove from the heat. Combine **75 g (½ cup) flour** and **15 g cornflour (cornstarch)** and stir into the hot liquid in one go using a wooden spoon. Heat for 1 minute, stirring continuously, until the dough forms into a ball that comes away from the saucepan bottom. Transfer the dough to a mixing bowl and mix in **2 medium-sized eggs** one at a time with the dough hook of an electric mixer, working at the highest speed. Grate **80 g mature, fully flavoured cheese** and knead into the dough together with ½ **tsp baking powder**. Preheat the oven to 200°C (390°F). Transfer the lukewarm mixture to a piping bag. Pipe about 35 hazelnut-sized portions onto a tray lined with baking paper. Bake in the preheated oven, middle rack, for 12–14 minutes.

GUACAMOLE WITH CAPSICUM & TOMATO SALSA (serves 4)

Halve **2 ripe avocados** and remove the seeds. Spoon the flesh from the skins, transfer to a mixing bowl and drizzle with the **juice of 1 lime** and **1 dash of salsa picante**. Season with **salt** and mash coarsely with a fork. Transfer to a tall, narrow container until serving. Push in an avocado seed and cover with cling wrap pressed right onto the surface to prevent any discolouring and preserve the beautiful green avocado colour.

Finely dice 1 green capsicum. Quarter, deseed and dice **2 tomatoes**. Peel and dice **1 red onion**. Combine everything and season with **1 dash white wine vinegar** and salt. Finely chop the leaves of **2 sprigs coriander** (cilantro) and toss with the vegetables.

Serve the guacamole with the capsicum and tomato salsa and **corn chips**.

— SAÚDE! —

An authentic capirinha!
(makes 1 glass, can be scaled up)

Trim the ends off **½ lime** and dice the lime. Crush the lime and **1–1.5 tsp white cane sugar** (alternatively another white sugar) with a muddler. Add **60 ml cachaça**, crushed ice or ice cubes (becoming more and more popular in Brazil, as the cocktail turns less watery). Shake for 15 seconds in a cocktail shaker or stir in a glass.

LINGÜIÇA COM CEBOLA ROXA E CACHAÇA, QUEIJO-DE-COALHO COM MELADO

and a virgin caipirinha

Two popular snacks from the Mocotó Bar e Restaurante in São Paulo are pork sausage with red onions, flambéed with cachaça, and cheese fried in ghee and served with molasses. These are my respectful interpretations.

LINGÜIÇA COM CEBOLA ROXA E CACHAÇA
(serves 4)

Lingüiça (or linguiça) is a coarse pork sausage quite similar to Italian salsiccia. However, this recipe also works well with chorizo or a coarse beef sausage. Slice about **300 g sausage**. Heat **1 tsp ghee** in a large non-stick pan over medium heat, add the sausage slices and fry until golden brown. Peel **1 red onion** and slice finely. Drizzle the sausage with **2 tbsp cachaça**. If you're game, hold a lit match to it for a dramatic flame. Extinguish the fire (by putting on a lid) and toss through the onion. Arrange on plates and serve sprinkled with freshly sliced **spring onion rings**.

QUEIJO-DE-COALHO COM MELADO
(serves 2–4)

North-eastern Brazil produces a salty cheese for frying that is similar to haloumi, which makes a good substitute. Slice **250 g haloumi**. Heat **2 tsp ghee** in a large non-stick pan over medium heat, add the cheese slices and fry until golden brown. Drizzle with **molasses** (dark sugar cane syrup, alternatively golden syrup) and serve with spicy, pickled sweet-and-sour **pimenta biquinho** (alternatively pickled **Peppadew** peppers).

SAÚDE!

How about a **virgin caipirinha**?

Trim the ends off **½ untreated lime** and dice the lime. Crush the lime and **1–1.5 tsp white cane sugar** (alternatively another white sugar) with a muddler. Add crushed ice or ice cubes and shake for 15 seconds in a cocktail shaker or stir in the glass. Top with chilled **lemonade or ginger ale**.

EMPANADAS DO BRASIL

INGREDIENTS

(makes about 35)

80 ml (⅓ cup) water

1 packet ground saffron (0.1 g)

350 g (2⅓ cups) flour (type 405, plus extra for dusting the benchtop)

50 g (3½ tbsp) butter, softened

50 g (3½ tbsp) lard

3 eggs (medium-sized)

1 dash vinegar

Salt

200 g cooked prawns

1 green capsicum (pepper)

1 small onion

3 tbsp olive oil

6 tbsp black beans (from a tin)

1 tomato

1 garlic clove

4 sprigs coriander (cilantro)

Chilli sauce (e.g. salsa picante or molho de pimenta verde)

Empanadas are a popular bar snack all over Latin America. I ate these spicy prawn empanadas with coriander at the counter of a corner café in São Paulo that combined a food stand, lunch restaurant and beer bar on a mere twenty square metres. It tasted delicious – about like this:

———

Heat the saffron in the water until the water turns yellow. Leave to cool. Combine the flour, butter, lard and 2 eggs with the saffron water, vinegar and a generous pinch of salt and knead to a smooth dough using a food processor. Wrap in cling wrap and set aside to rest.

Meanwhile, chop the prawns. Finely dice the capsicum; peel and finely dice the onion. Heat the oil in a frying pan over medium heat and sauté both until soft, about 4–5 minutes. Rinse the beans and drain in a sieve. Cut the tomato into eights, finely dice and toss with the beans. Peel and mince the garlic and coarsely chop the coriander. Add both to the pan together with the chopped prawns and mix through. Season with salt and chilli sauce to taste. Leave to cool.

Meanwhile, roll out the dough about 0.5 cm thick on a lightly floured surface. Cut out rounds of about 9 cm diameter. Knead leftover dough together, roll out again and cut out more rounds. Repeat until you have used up the dough. Preheat the oven to 200°C (390°F). Divide the filling among the dough circles using a teaspoon.

Whisk the remaining egg with 2 tbsp water and brush the dough edges thinly with the mixture. Fold the pastry over the filling to make semicircles. Press the edges firmly together to seal and use a fork to create serrated edges. Transfer the empanadas to a tray lined with baking paper. Brush with the remaining egg wash. Bake in the preheated oven, middle rack, until golden brown, about 20–25 minutes. Serve lukewarm.

MUSIC: *Any best-of album by Vinícius de Moraes, all through the night. The probably best-known work by this Brazilian singer, poet, diplomat and bon vivant are the Portuguese/Spanish original lyrics of the world hit "The Girl from Ipanema". His comprehensive musical legacy deserves to be rediscovered.*

USA

Bialys are similar to bagels, but they have
a little well in the middle instead of a hole,
which is filled with braised or fried onions.

BIALYS

INGREDIENTS

(makes 8 bialys)

For the dough:

15 g fresh yeast

250 g (1⅔ cups) flour (type 405,
    plus extra for the benchtop)

150 g (1 cup) buckwheat flour

340 ml (1⅓ cups) water

1 tsp sugar

½ tsp salt

Braised onions:

2 onions

1 tbsp oil

Salt

1 pinch sugar

50 ml (¼ cup) apple juice

Freshly ground black pepper

Flour for dusting

For the salmon salad:

250 g salmon fillet, deboned

2 tbsp olive oil

Salt

1 small red onion

1–2 tsp capers

1 tbsp white wine vinegar

3–4 tbsp mayonnaise

A little rocket

MUSIC: *In 1996, the Beastie Boys recorded "The In Sound from Way Out!", an instrumental album that is still somewhat of an insider tip. It features a number of great jazz and 70s funk songs that groove along perfectly for the twilight hour.*

Bialys, a specialty of Jewish-American cooking, are incredibly popular in New York City, although they originally come from the Polish town of Bialystok. These small bread rolls are traditionally served warm, spread with a little butter, to have with coffee, but in New York they have been updated with rich fillings such as roast beef, pastrami, salmon or salmon salad.

———————

The evening before, prepare a starter dough from 5 g yeast, 30 g flour, 50 g buckwheat flour and 100 ml (½ cup) water. Cover with a clean kitchen towel and leave to prove at room temperature overnight. The next day, combine the remaining flour with sugar and salt. Stir the remaining yeast into 240 ml (1 cup) lukewarm water and add to the flour, together with the starter dough. Knead with the dough hook of a food processor or electric mixer at medium speed for about 5 minutes. Cover and set aside to rise for 1 hour.

Meanwhile, slice the onions into rings. Heat the oil in a large frying pan, add the onion rings, season with salt and braise over medium heat until soft and golden brown, about 12–15 minutes. Stir in the sugar, deglaze with apple juice and bring to a boil. Season with pepper and adjust the seasoning.

Preheat the oven to 200°C (390°F). Divide the dough into 8 even portions and shape each portion into a ball. Leave to rise for 30 minutes. Make a well in the centre of each ball. Fill with the braised onions and dust the onions lightly with flour. Transfer the bialys to a tray lined with baking paper and bake in the preheated oven for 15–20 minutes.

Heat the oil in a frying pan and fry the salmon 6–8 minutes on each side. Season with salt and pull coarsely apart. Peel and finely dice the red onion and toss with the capers. Season with vinegar and salt and mix with the pulled salmon. Slice the bialys open, add a little mayonnaise and top with salmon salad and rocket.

THE COLOURFUL CULINARY HERITAGE OF THE USA

SUNSET WITH A VIEW

Some swear by Mallory Square in Key West, Florida. Others love the sunset at Hopi Point in the Grand Canyon National Park. But... the best US sunsets will always be found in Technicolor (a must!) at the end of old westerns.

DEVILS ON HORSEBACK

RUMAKI

It's not quite clear who or what exactly is supposed to be devilish about this tasty mixture of port wine-soaked prunes and blue vein cheese wrapped in bacon – on the contrary, these delightful little snacks taste rather divine. Speaking of divine: there's also angels on horseback, another popular American (and British) bar food, which is oysters wrapped in crispy bacon.

In 1937, the waitress Cora Irene Sund fell in love with the barkeeper Ernest Raymond Beaumont-Gantt, who was very fond of the emerging tiki culture, at the time the pop culture expression of US Americans' longing for Polynesian/Hawaiian exoticism. The couple opened Hollywood's first themed restaurant, Don the Beachcomber, which had lavishly decorated dining rooms named "The Black Hole of Calcutta" and "The Cannibal Room", among others. The restaurant served cocktails with similarly colourful names between Maori torches, timber tiki carvings, sharks' teeth and artificial palm trees, and their bar food too was rather imaginative. The rumaki snacks invented by Beaumont-Gantt still form part of the US culinary canon.

HERE'S HOW (makes 12)

Soak **12 pitted prunes** in 3 tbsp water and **4 tbsp red port wine** overnight. The next day, drain the prunes and stuff them with a small piece of **blue vein cheese, 100 g** in total. Halve **6 slices bacon**. Wrap each stuffed prune with a strip of bacon and transfer to a tray lined with baking paper. Bake for 15–20 minutes in the preheated oven (180°C (350°F) fan-forced, 200°C (390°F) conventional) until the bacon is nicely browned.

HERE'S HOW (makes 12)

Wash and trim **200 g chicken liver** and cut into 12 even pieces. Marinate in **1 tbsp sweet soy sauce** and **½ tsp freshly grated ginger**. Drain **12 water chestnuts** from a tin and marinate in **2 tbsp sherry**. Halve **6 slices bacon**. Wrap 1 water chestnut and 1 piece of chicken liver each into ½ bacon strip and hold in place with toothpicks. Bake for 15–20 minutes in the preheated oven (180°C (350°F) fan-forced, 200°C (390°F) conventional) until the bacon is nicely browned.

—— CHEERS! ——

This goes perfectly with well chilled white or red port, but also tastes great with a nice glass of beer or your favourite (semi-dry) wine. Oloroso or manzanilla sherry are also excellent choices!

NON-ALCOHOLIC: chilled grape juice.

NACHOS

INGREDIENTS

(serves 4)

2 onions

1 garlic clove

4 tbsp olive oil

500 g mince

1 tbsp sweet paprika powder

1 pinch smoked paprika powder
 (pimentón de la vera)

1 tbsp golden syrup

2 tbsp tomato paste

1 tin diced tomatoes

Salt

1 red onion

1 spring onion

1 avocado

1–2 tsp vinegar

1 tbsp olive oil

About 300 g corn chips

200 g (2 cups) grated cheddar
 cheese

Jalapeños to taste

MUSIC: *The Fun Lovin' Criminals are three cool guys from New York who feel at home in hoodies as much as in pinstripe suits. Their 1998 album "100% Colombian" delivers elegant swing with an irresistible mixture of cool jazz, R&B, solid funk, a pinch of rock and blue-s, plus relaxed rap delivered in a husky voice.*

CHEERS!

Enjoy with an ice-cold cerveza such as a Pacifico, Sol or Corona, or any refreshing, chilled summer cocktail of choice.

Ignacio "Nacho" Anaya, a chef at the Victory Club in Piedras Negras, Mexico, is believed to have invented "nachos especiales". At least that's how he named the dish he first served to a group of Texan women waiting for their food in 1943. It was a small selection of everything he happened to have at hand: corn chips, Wisconsin cheddar and pickled jalapeño chillies. About 20 years later, in 1964, Sal Manriquez and his wife Margarita came up with the idea to sell broken and leftover corn chips done up with beans, a spicy sauce, jalapeños and cheese, at the annual state fair in Dallas, 400 miles (650 kms) from Piedras Negras. Their Margarita's State Fair Nachos were a hit, and Manriquez launched into big nacho business. In 1975 he applied for a licence for selling nachos in the Arlington baseball stadium but was rejected. However, the stadium started selling its own Ballpark Nachos brand of corn chips with cheese soon after, which became famous all over the US.

———

Peel and finely dice the onions; peel and mince the garlic. Heat some olive oil in a frying pan and cook both until soft, about 4–6 minutes. Add the mince and fry until crumbly. Dust with the two paprika powders and stir in the golden syrup and tomato paste. Add the diced tomatoes. Refill the empty tin with water and also add. Season with salt and simmer, uncovered, over low heat for 20–25 minutes to thicken, stirring occasionally.

Preheat the oven to 200°C (390°F). Peel and halve the red onion and slice finely. Chop the spring onion into fine rings. Halve the avocado and remove the seed. Spoon out the flesh and dice. Marinate the vegetables in vinegar and olive oil and season with salt.

Layer the corn chips with the hot mince sauce, grated cheese and avocado and onion mixture, on a tray lined with baking paper. Briefly heat in the oven for 6–8 minutes. Serve immediately with jalapeño chillies.

HOME-MADE TONIC
to serve with your favourite gin

BASIC TONIC

(makes about 1 litre)

2 organic limes

1 organic lemon

2 organic mandarins
or 1 organic orange

3 sticks lemongrass

30 g cinchona bark (order online)

25 g vitamin C powder (pure
L-ascorbic acid)

500 g (2¼ cups) sugar

I have developed a basic tonic as a sophisticated, subtle accompaniment that clearly concentrates on two core elements of any good tonic: a bitter note (from the cinchona bark) and lemony freshness. That's all you need to allow your gin to shine! The third, decisive element in a gin & tonic is carbonation – use your favourite soda or sparkling mineral water for this. You'll have three elements to play with to find your perfect personal blend. I'm quite fond of a mixture of 40–60 ml home-made tonic syrup per 60 ml of my favourite gin. On ice, obviously, and topped up with sparkling mineral water to taste. I personally prefer water with not-so-fine bubbles.

———————

Fill a large twist-top jar with 500 ml (2 cups) water. Finely grate the citrus fruit zest with a microplane, avoiding the bitter white pith, and stir into the water immediately. Finely slice the lemongrass and add to the mixture together with the cinchona bark and vitamin C powder. Leave the mixture to develop its flavours in a warm place (near a heater, on a sunny windowsill) for 24 hours.

Bring 300 ml (1¼ cups) water to a boil with the sugar and boil vigorously for 5 minutes. Set aside to cool fully. Strain the tonic mixture through a fine muslin cloth or coffee filter and combine with the cooled sugar syrup. Fill the tonic mixture into clean twist-top jars. It'll keep for at least 2–3 weeks in your refrigerator.

TIP: Try your next G&T in a wide wine glass for a sophisticated look that also allows the flavours and aromas to develop better than in a long drink glass.

MEXICO

The Spanish/American word "enchilada" means "stuffed with chilli".
Back in 1949, the American Dialect Society complained
in its newsletter that enchiladas were nothing but "a Mexican dish,
prepared more for *turistas* than for local consumption".
We don't mind being tourists in this case!

CHICKEN & CHORIZO ENCHILADAS

INGREDIENTS

(makes 8 enchiladas)

½ **roast chicken (ready-made)**

1 **tin black beans (425 g net weight)**

2 **chorizo sausages**

3 **tbsp olive oil**

800 ml (3¼ cups) salsa roja (p. 229)

Salt

Chilli sauce

8 **large tortillas**

200 g (1½ cups) Monterey Jack **or cheddar cheese**

50 g (⅓ cup) feta

4 **tomatoes, mixed or all red**

1 **small red onion**

4 **sprigs coriander (cilantro)**

1 **tbsp white wine vinegar**

150 ml (⅔ cup)sour cream

Pull the chicken meat, including the skin, off the bone in bite-sized pieces. Rinse the beans under cold water and drain. Finely dice the chorizo. Heat 1 tbsp olive oil in a large non-stick pan and fry the chicken and chorizo for 3–5 minutes. Add the beans and about a third of the salsa roja. Season with salt and chilli sauce to taste.

Preheat the oven to 200°C (390°F). Divide the chilli mixture among the tortillas and roll the tortillas up. Spread a little of the remaining salsa across the bottom of a baking dish. Transfer the enchiladas to the dish and cover with the remaining salsa. Sprinkle with the grated cheese and crumbled feta and bake in the preheated oven for 25–30 minutes.

Meanwhile, quarter, deseed and dice the tomatoes. Peel and finely dice the onion. Chop the coriander and combine with the tomatoes and onions in a bowl. Toss with the vinegar and 2 tbsp olive oil and season with salt. Remove the enchiladas from the oven. Top with the fresh tomato salsa, drizzle with sour cream and serve.

MUSIC: *"Welcome to Tijuana"! A particularly good version was produced by the band Amparanola ("Buen Rollito") with their singer Amparo Sánchez!*

TORTAS AHOGADAS

INGREDIENTS

(makes 4 rolls)

450 ml (1¾ cups) salsa roja (p. 229)

Lime juice

White wine vinegar

4 birote or crusty rolls
   or burger buns

250 g green cabbage

Red chilli to taste

Salt

Sugar

Olive oil

½ roast chicken (ready-made)

Ground allspice

Ground coriander (cilantro)

Drunken rolls? This recipe is no joke, though: these *tortas ahogadas* rather taste divine, rich and juicy with a stuffing of tender meat and a drowning quantity of salsa roja. They're messy eating that's blissful and filling. In Mexico, they are served in crusty, white birote rolls. Use any type of crusty white roll as a substitutes for the original; alternatively use lightly toasted burger buns.

———

Season the salsa roja with lime juice and vinegar to taste and heat. Warm the rolls or buns in the oven at 80°C (175°F). Slice the cabbage and chilli thinly. Season both with salt and a pinch of sugar and massage until soft. Toss with a dash of vinegar and 1 tbsp olive oil.

Pull the chicken (with the skin) off the bone into bite-sized pieces. Heat 1–2 tbsp olive oil in a large non-stick pan, add the chicken and fry for 3–5 minutes. Season with salt and a touch of ground allspice and coriander. Stir in 4 tbsp salsa roja. Remove the rolls or buns from the oven and slice open. Top with the pulled chicken, cabbage salad and salsa roja and serve.

MUSIC: *The Mexican singer and multi-instrumentalist Rana Santacruz from Brooklyn, New York, published his album "Por Ahí", a celebration of traditional Mexican music without a hint of folklore, in 2015. He calls his music Mexican bluegrass and Irish mariachi, mixes it with jazz and Balkan beats – and it all goes together wonderfully.*

¡SALUD!

May I suggest a classic **Paloma**?

Fill a long drink glass with ice cubes, add a pinch of salt and squeeze 1–2 lime quarters on top. Top with 50 ml blanco tequila and 150 ml ice-cold grapefruit lemonade.

NON-ALCOHOLIC: as above, but with 1 tsp agave syrup instead of the tequila.

CHILAQUILES

A Mexican breakfast and excellent way of using up leftovers that's delicious at any time of the day or evening. Slice leftover tortillas into strips. Transfer to a baking dish, top with tomato salsa and cheese and bake. Serve with cucumber and coriander (cilantro) salsa, fried eggs, avocado and onions. Note that this dish hinges on the quality of the salsa roja, which is used in all recipes in this chapter.

SALSA ROJA
(makes about 1.4 l)

This sauce can be easily prepared in large quantities. It'll taste even better, and it can be refrigerated for several days or even frozen.

Peel and finely dice **300 g onions** and season with **salt**. Heat **6 tbsp olive oil** in a saucepan over low heat, add the onions and sauté until soft, about 5 minutes. Meanwhile, quarter **1 red and 1 green chilli** lengthwise. Deseed if you like a milder taste and mince. Peel and mince **2 cloves garlic**. Add the chilli and garlic, **4 tbsp agave syrup**, **2 tbsp sweet paprika powder** and **1 pinch smoked paprika powder (pimentón de la vera)** to the onions. Stir in **3 tins diced tomatoes (425 g net weight each)** and 450 ml (1¾ cups) water. Season with salt. Simmer gently, uncovered, over low heat for about 30 minutes. Stir occasionally. Mash the salsa coarsely with a hand-held blender and continue to simmer for another 15 minutes, uncovered.

SALSA VERDE (serves 4)

Dice **200 g organic cucumber, 1 mild green chilli, 2 spring onions** and **½ green capsicum**. Combine with **1 bunch coriander, 1 bunch parsley, 6–8 tbsp oil** and **1 tbsp roasted, salted peanuts** in a blender and blend until creamy. Season with a **dash of lime juice** and **salt**.

CHILAQUILES (serves 4)

Slice **3 small tortillas** per person into strips about 2–3 cm wide. Cover the bottom of a large baking dish with about **6–8 tbsp salsa roja** and arrange the tortilla strips in loose loops on top. Top with more salsa roja. Sprinkle with **100 g (1 cup) grated cheddar cheese** and **60–80 g (½ cup) crumbled feta cheese**. Bake in the preheated oven (200°C / 390°F) for 12–15 minutes. Meanwhile, heat a little **oil** in a frying pan and fry **1–2 eggs** per person. Season with **salt**. Peel **1 red onion** and slice into rings. Remove the baking dish from the oven. Peel and slice **1 avocado**; season both with salt and a few dashes of **vinegar** and arrange on top of the baked dish. Drizzle with **salsa verde**, garnish with a **handful of coriander leaves** and serve with the fried eggs.

¡SALUD!

Mexicans have this with black coffee in the morning. Enjoy with a Mexican beer for the end of the day.

NON-ALCOHOLIC: "El Blandengue" – pineapple juice and a little honey on ice, seasoned with a touch of cinnamon and a dash of lime juice.

FIN!

RECIPE INDEX

STEVAN'S THANK-YOUS

AUSTRALIA

Our indigenous friend Josh "Koomal" Whiteland, who introduced us to Aboriginal culture and took us to Ngilgi Cave.

KOOMALDREAMING.COM.AU

The Australian TV chef and artist Poh Ling Yeow, who shared so much about culinary trends in Australia with me.

POHLINGYEOW.COM

Jim Mendolia (Fremantle Sardine Company), who took us out fishing for sardines.

FREMANTLESARDINE.COM.AU

BRAZIL

The team at the São Paulo Goethe Institute, above all my hostess, Stefanie Kastner, and my guides to culinary Brazil, Danilo Narciso, Ana Rüsche and Danilo Rolim.

MENUCONTENT.COM.BR
WORDPRESS.ANARUSCHE.COM

JAPAN

The grand masters Nagano-san, Tetsuya Saotome and Zaiyu Hasegawa, who shared insights into Japanese food philosophy with us.

PORTUGAL

Maria Santos and the team at Cabeça de Cabra for their hospitality, delightful food and culinary tips.

CABECADACABRA.COM

SPAIN

The photographer Günter Beer and his family, who provided me with a key to both Spanish cuisine and my small migrant worker casita. Thank you for your hospitality over all these past years.

BEERFOTO.COM

AUSTRIA

The team of Christian Brandstätter Verlag and my colleague Katharina Seiser, who always knows where to find Austrian cooking at its best.

ESSKULTUR.AT

DANIELA'S THANK-YOUS

**EVERYBODY WHO HAS PROVIDED
US WITH TIPS AND OPENED DOORS**

Aviel Avdar, DRS Delight Rental Services; Justin Blackford, Foodloose, foodloosetours.com.au; Gotthard Bauer, Yallingup Woodfired Bread; Bayern Tourismus Marketing GmbH; Thorsten Bieling; Betül Cacan; Clever Little Taylor; Agnes Farkas, Callas Café & Restaurant; Matthias Felsner, Martin Fetz, Philipp Haufler, Hubert Peter, rien; Fiaker Paul; Fremantle Sardine Company; Peter C. Friese, Hans-Jürgen Serloth, Lukas Breitenecker, Zum Schwarzen Kameel; Sofia Gabriel, Comer O Mundo; Zsombor Gál, Hungarian Tourism Agency; Golvet; Juri Gottschall; Grupo Multifood; Jon Guinea, Hopwater Distribution; Tamara Hirsch, Nihonbashi; Juri Kobayashi; Kumami Berlin; Heidi Leipold, Amrit; Mariana Marques, José Avillez, Grupo José Avillez; André Marques Santos, Amuse Bouche; Zsofi Mautner, chiliesvanilia.hu; Joerg Meyer, Le Lion; Bernd Müller; Jessie Nicely, compound-butter. com; Clint Nolan, Kate Wilkinson, Lavish Habits; Èva Oláh, Fricska Gastropub; Chloe Pressman, Tracy Smyth, Bellota Restaurant; Áron Reményik, Bock Bisztro; Ulrike Schillo; Schoilmichl; Holger Sturm, Annette Hoppe, Tanja Müller, Cafè Paris; Tanja and Oliver Trific; Claudia Winkler-Görbe, the Hungarian embassy in Berlin; Jörg Zabel, Gasthaus Zum Nußbaum.

**EVERYBODY WHO AGREED TO HAVE
THEIR PHOTOS PUBLISHED**

Benjamin Becker, Cseko, Csaba Csongràdi, Gàbor Dneghiciu, Miguel Dumas, Susanne Eckert, Arash Ghalavand, Fábio Guerreiro, Ammiel Holder, Kuma Kenta, Linus Klein, Sorya A. Laalem, Erna Lenhardt, Francesco Manzoni, Jim Mendolia, Robert Neiger, Manfred Panzmann, Jasmina Poljakovif, Alister Robertson, Kathariana Schleider, Pablo Schomburg, Bruna Simoes, Jaskaran Singh, Sandeep Singh, Frederico Vargas, Martin Wagner.

PHOTO SESSIONS AT DUSK

TEAM

STEVAN PAUL — *concept, text, recipes & food styling*

In this book, Stevan Paul follows the course of the setting sun once around the world. His drink at dusk is the Port Tonic on p. 222. His street food best seller, "Auf die Hand", his innovative alfresco cookbook "Open Air" and the first cookbook on trendy craft beers have been published by Brandstätter.

STEVANPAUL.DE

DANIELA HAUG — *photography*

The work on this book has taken Daniela Haug on a photographic journey to sunsets between Padua and San Francisco. In Lisbon, she not only rediscovered her love for pastèis de nata (p. 192), but also found a new favourite spot on the Ponto Final. She is a passionate photographer of people, food and travels and works internationally for publishers, agencies and companies.

DANIELAHAUG.DE

MIRIAM STROBACH — *visual design*

The moment between day and night has something magical. This is where glamour happens! Miriam Strobach loves to celebrate this moment with her own creation: "Kalê" herb liqueur with lemon on ice. She develops and designs food and drinks projects as a designer and co-founder of Le Foodink.

LE FOODINK.AT | KALE.AT

ELSE RIEGER — *Editor*

Else Rieger, German by birth, Viennese by choice, discovered her love for the blue hour as a child, long before she became interested in cookbooks. These days, she loves spending the sunset somewhere near water. Unfortunately, that's not always possible, so her home screen shows the sunset at the Ligurian coast.